LIFE IN TH ... RIT
OF JE ...

(THE BOOK FOR LIFE AND ... ON)

This book offers understanding the true knowledge of love, which is the source of life and inspiration for personal, community, industrial, trade, business and management development and reconstruction and for improving the quality of life and happiness worldwide. The theme is derived from the love revolution of our Lord Jesus Christ. *through the Scriptures.* This engaging book can help everyone to experience sense and stability out of the world of confusion of the whole human race. The message is constructive and it transcends every human culture of servitude to ignorance, sin and death.

JUBILEE A. D. 2000
COMMEMORATIVE EDITION
AMP
Ave Maria Publishers Limited

LIFE IN THE HOLY SPIRIT OF JESUS CHRIST

(THE BOOK FOR LIFE AND INSPIRATION FOR RECONSTRUCTION)

" Whoever has seen me has seen the Father " Jn 14:19
My commandment is this: love one another, just as I love you. '

JUBILEE A. D. 2000
COMMEMORATIVE EDITION
AMP
Ave Maria Publishers Limited

LIFE IN THE HOLY SPIRIT OF JESUS CHRIST

(THE BOOK FOR LIFE AND INSPIRATION FOR RECONSTRUCTION)

**"I am the Way: I am Truth and Life.
No one can come to the Father except through me."
(Jn 14: 6) JB**

**JUBILEE A. D. 2000
COMMEMORATIVE EDITION
AMP**

Ave Maria Publishers Limited

LIFE IN THE HOLY SPIRIT OF JESUS CHRIST

(THE BOOK FOR LIFE AND INSPIRATION FOR RECONSTRUCTION)

"Everything is possible for God"
Mark 10: 27

JUBILEE A. D. 2000
COMMEMORATIVE EDITION
AMP

Ave Maria Publishers Limited

LIFE IN THE HOLY SPIRIT OF JESUS CHRIST

(THE BOOK FOR LIFE AND INSPIRATION FOR RECONSTRUCTION)

"Do you not believe that I am in the Father and the Father is in me? What I say to you I do not speak of my own accord: it is the Father, living in me, who is doing his works."

"Whoever holds to my commandments and keeps them is the one who loves me; and whoever loves me will be loved by my Father, and I shall love him and reveal myself to him"

(Jn 14: 10, 21) JB

JUBILEE A. D. 2000
COMMEMORATIVE EDITION
AMP

Ave Maria Publishers Limited

LIFE IN THE HOLY SPIRIT OF JESUS CHRIST

(THE BOOK FOR LIFE AND INSPIRATION FOR RECONSTRUCTION)

"I am with you always; yes, to the end of time"
Mat 28: 20 JB

JUBILEE A. D. 2000
COMMEMORATIVE EDITION
AMP
Ave Maria Publishers Limited

LIFE IN THE HOLY SPIRIT OF JESUS CHRIST

(THE BOOK FOR LIFE AND INSPIRATION FOR RECONSTRUCTION)

"The Holy Spirit, whom the Father will send in my name, will teach you everything and remind you of all I have said to you."
(Jn 14: 26) JB

JUBILEE A. D. 2000
COMMEMORATIVE EDITION
AMP

Ave Maria Publishers Limited

LIFE IN THE HOLY SPIRIT OF JESUS CHRIST

(THE BOOK FOR LIFE AND INSPIRATION FOR RECONSTRUCTION)

FAMILY RECORD

THIS BOOK BELONGS TO:____________________

CONTACT ADDRESS:____________________

PARISH CHURCH:____________________

ADDRESS:____________________

DATE OF BIRTH:____________________

DATE OF BAPTISM:____________________

DATE OF CONFIRMATION:____________________

NAME OF SPOUSE:____________________

DATE OF MARRIAGE:____________________

NAME OF CHILDREN:____________________

"Why do you call me, "Lord, Lord," and yet don't do what I tell you?"
Luke 6:46

JUBILEE A. D. 2000
COMMEMORATIVE EDITION
AMP

Ave Maria Publishers Limited

LIFE IN THE HOLY SPIRIT OF JESUS CHRIST

(THE BOOK FOR LIFE AND INSPIRATION FOR RECONSTRUCTION)

"If you obey my commands, you will remain in my love, just as I have obeyed my Father 's commands and remain in his love. I have told you this so that my joy may be in you and that your joy may be complete. My commandment is this: love one another, just as I love you.

The greatest love a person can have for his friends is to give his life for them. And you are my friends if you do what I command you.

I do not call you servants any longer, because servants do not know what their master is doing. Instead, I call you friends, because I have told you everything I have heard from my Father.

You did not choose me; I chose you and appointed you to go and bear much fruit, the kind of fruit that endures. And so the Father will give you whatever you ask of him in my name. This, then, is what I command you: love one another."
(Jn 15: 10-17)

JUBILEE A. D. 2000
COMMEMORATIVE EDITION
AMP

Ave Maria Publishers Limited

LIFE IN THE HOLY SPIRIT OF JESUS CHRIST

(THE BOOK FOR LIFE AND INSPIRATION FOR RECONSTRUCTION)

"And eternal life means knowing you, the only true God, and knowing Jesus Christ, whom you sent."
Jn 17: 3

JUBILEE A. D. 2000
COMMEMORATIVE EDITION
AMP

Ave Maria Publishers Limited

LIFE IN THE HOLY SPIRIT OF JESUS CHRIST

(THE BOOK FOR LIFE AND INSPIRATION FOR RECONSTRUCTION)

By

ROBERT K GLAH, LL M; Ph D. [LONDON]

of the Inner Temple, Barrister;

Solicitor and Advocate of the Superior Courts of Justice, Ghana

JUBILEE A. D. 2000

COMMEMORATIVE EDITION

AMP

Ave Maria Publishers Limited

Published in the United Kingdom by
Ave Maria Publishers Limited
153 Temple Chambers, Temple Avenue
London EC4Y OHP

Tel: 020 7353 0133
Fax: 020 7353 0533

Website: www.avemariapublishersbooks.org.uk
E-mail: book@avemariapublishersbooks.org.uk

First published December 2000

ISBN 1 903519-02-0 Softcover

Nihil obstat	Father Anton Cowan
Imprimatur	Rt. Rev. Patrick O'Donoghue, V.G. Bishop in West London
Westminister	25th September 2000

The Nihil obstat and Imprimatur are a declaration that a book or pamphlet is considered to be free from doctrinal or moral error. It is not implied that those who have granted the Nihil obstat and Imprimatur agree with the contents, opinions or statements expressed.

Net proceeds of sale of this book will be used to promote general charitable purposes throughout the world and in particular to provide financial and other assistance for the advancement of education as the trustees of Human Freedom in their absolute discretion may from time to time determine. Human Freedom is an international charity incorporated in the United Kingdom with limited liability by guarantee Registration Number 3087036 Charity Commission Reg. No. 1049216.

Typeset by the Lavenham Press Limited
Printed and bound in Slovak Republic

MY PRAYER FOR YOU

In the name of the Father, and of the Son, and of the Holy Spirit. Amen.

MAY OUR LORD JESUS CHRIST speak to you and touch you through his Words in this book.

MAY HE BLESS you and enlighten you so that you can see the new vision for the liberation of the whole human race from the Evil One and for the improvement of the quality of life of the entire human race worldwide.

MAY HE BLESS you with his peace, which enables all understanding.

MAY HE BLESS all the faithful and the priests at St Joseph's Catholic Church, Leyton, London.

MAY HE BLESS all members of my family and friends who waited for almost forty years for the inspiring Words of our Lord Jesus Christ in *Life in the Holy Spirit of Jesus Christ* and in particular my daughter, Divina, who helped me whilst typing the manuscript and my sons, Richard, who was my research assistant on the Words of our Lord, David, Philip and Charles for their help.

MAY HE BLESS all those who purchase and use this book and share with me the new vision, self-renewal and life in the Holy Spirit of Jesus Christ, and support our Charity Appeal for funds through the purchase of this book to enable Human freedom to carry out its human rights and general charitable objectives and activities throughout the world.

MAY HE BLESS and enlighten all heads of states and governments and all community leaders worldwide.

MAY HE BLESS and send his Holy Spirit to give understanding to all young men and women worldwide

MAY HE BLESS and enlighten all my learned friends at the Bar and judges worldwide and in particular my learned friends at the English

Bar in the Catholic Lawyers Association, London.
MAY HE BLESS and guide the whole human race and send us his Holy Spirit to tell us what we ought to do and how to do it and to awake to do it.

MAY HE BLESS and guide his Church and unite all members of the Christian churches of every denomination and in particular His Holiness, Pope John Paul II, the Head of the Catholic Church, the Vicar of Christ, servant of servants of God.

MAY HE GUIDE the whole human race to experience his love for the whole human race and grant our prayers for inspiration and reconstruction worldwide for the happiness of the whole human race.

MAY HE GIVE peace, light, happiness and everlasting life to all our brothers and sisters who departed from this world with the hope of rising in body, soul and spirit. Lord, we trust in your love and mercy. Do not look on our sins, but on the faith of your Church, and grant us forgiveness, the peace and unity of your Kingdom, where you live forever and ever in your world without end.

GLORY BE to the Father, and to the Son, and to the Holy Spirit.
As it was in the beginning,
is now, and ever shall be,
world without end.

THROUGH HIM, with him, in him, in the Unity of the Holy Spirit, all glory and honour is yours, Almighty Father, for ever and ever. Amen.

ACKNOWLEDGEMENTS

The Catechism of the Catholic Church, published in Ireland by Veritas 1994 inspired the publication of this book for the use of Christians and non-Christians worldwide.

Scriptures quoted from the Good News Bible Second Edition Copyright 1994 published by The Bible Societies/Harper Collins Publishers Ltd, UK, Copyright American Bible Society, 1966, 1971, 1976, 1992.

Extracts from the English translation of the Roman Missal, copyright 1973, International Committee on English in the Liturgy, Inc All rights reserved.

The Apostles' Creed and the Nicene Creed, copyright International Consultation on English Texts.

The Hail Mary, The Prayer of St Francis of Assisi, Hail Holy Queen and The Baptismal Promises were taken from Prayers Everyone Should Know. ST PAULS, Middlegreen, Slough SL3 6BT, United Kingdom. Copyright ST PAULS.

The image of our Lord Jesus Christ on the cover and inside the book is reproduced from an Italian postcard.

The political map of the world is reproduced by permission of Oxford Cartographers.

The Publishers hope that no copyright has been infringed. Forgiveness is sought with apology if it proves otherwise; corrections will be made in a reprint.

PUBLISHERS' RECOMMENDATION

Many people are taking an increasing interest in the principles of Christianity as tools for guiding people for inspiration for reconstruction and for improving the quality of life worldwide. Thus, "Life in the Holy Spirit of Jesus Christ" has concisely brought home to everyone in any family, trade, profession, vocation and employment the enduring principles of the Good News of Love from God and salvation of the whole human race from human culture of servitude to ignorance, sin and death through Jesus Christ for inspiration and reconstruction worldwide. The Love of God for the whole human race is stronger than human culture of servitude to ignorance, sin and death.

The Good News is for self-renewal, personal development, reconstruction, happiness and for improving the quality of life of people worldwide. Love is constructive. Love renews the world through Christ.

The wondrous principles of life in the Spirit of Christ, *through the Scriptures*, are presented on the basis of faith in God and in Jesus Christ for self-renewal. Self-renewal is the wisdom of making holy one 's physical, mental, emotional and spiritual nature in union with Christ in order to receive more energy and the grace of God and to respond effectively to one 's daily responsibilities. Christ never deceives and cannot be deceived by anyone. You must be perfect, just as your Father in heaven is perfect!

Through the empowerment of the Holy Spirit, the author, Dr. Robert Kwao Glah, a servant of God, and a man of law and order, reveals that the Creator endows every human being with certain inalienable human rights and fundamental freedoms; among these are the right to *Life in the Holy Spirit of Jesus Christ* and *inspiration* for personal development, reconstruction and happiness worldwide. Jesus Christ is the same from the beginning, today and forever.

The content of this book is divided into five interrelated parts as follows. *Freedom to choose, self-knowledge, human culture of servitude to sin and death and salvation through the love of God for the whole human race. *The profession of the Christian faith, nature of God and the Most Holy Trinity. *The principles of managing industry, trade and commerce for reward with confidence in the context of the Holy Spirit. *Human freedom in the Spirit of Jesus Christ in the context of human nature, the Lord 's Sermon on the Mount and the Ten Commandments and human rights. *Nature and power of prayer, Baptism, Confirmation, the Eucharist, the power of Reconciliation, Anointing the Sick for health and healing, Marriage and the family, Holy Orders and Christian funeral. All roads lead to human freedom from the culture of servitude to sin and death to enable personal development, reconstruction, happiness and protection of human rights worldwide. Love is creative.

Use this book to know and experience direct the truth, which shall set you free from human culture of servitude to sin and death for personal happiness. Knowledge is power.

Study this book for thirty to sixty minutes daily whilst the door is shut. Put the principles into practice every day. This will help you to generate more energy and tranquillity of body, mind, emotions and spirit within yourself and around to enable you to respond effectively to personal management of your daily responsibilities.

The publishers recommend purchase and use of this book by everyone in order to raise money for charity and to spread the Good News of Jesus Christ for personal happiness and reconstruction. Recommend use of this book to your friends at work, at home and abroad so that all of us may share in the joy and happiness of Christ. Love one another.

Ave Maria Publishers Limited
153 Temple Chambers
London EC4Y OHP

1st November 2000
Jubilee A. D. 2000
Commemorative Edition

LIFE IN THE HOLY SPIRIT OF JESUS CHRIST

(THE BOOK FOR LIFE AND INSPIRATION FOR RECONSTRUCTION)

**"Human beings cannot live on bread alone,
but need every word that God speaks."
Matt. 4:4 GNB**

Overall, this book is based on the love revolution of Jesus Christ, *through the Scriptures*, for constructive personal development and inspiration for reconstruction. It is not a biography of the author but a sharing of the love of God for the whole human race, through "*Life in the Holy Spirit of Jesus Christ*". Its message transcends every denominational, religious, political and national boundary. In this context, this book is addressed to students, youngsters and people worldwide for inspiration for reconstruction in their own corner.

The love of God for the whole human race through Christ is stronger than human culture of servitude to ignorance, sin and death.

**JUBILEE A. D. 2000
COMMEMORATIVE EDITION
AMP**

Ave Maria Publishers Limited

Table of Contents

My Prayer for You xiii

Acknowledgements xv

Publishers' Recommendation xvi

Introduction 1

Purpose of this book
What is the Christian meaning of Love?
The Love of Jesus Christ is stronger than human culture of ignorance of God, sin and death.
Self-Renewal for Personal Development, Reconstruction and Happiness.
Coverage of this book
The Spirit driving the research and publishing of this book in the context of UN policy.
Who should use this book?
How to use this book
Table of Followers of all Faiths Worldwide.

PART ONE

FREEDOM TO CHOOSE
IN THE CONTEXT OF THE SCRIPTURES

1. **Principles of Self-knowledge** 26

The search for happiness. What is self-renewal? Self-knowledge. Responsibilities. Conscience. Imagination. Will power. Leadership. Management. Courage. Abundance. Trust. Mysteries and Responses of the risen Lord Jesus Christ. Know the cause within yourself and use your talent for reconstruction.

2. **Freedom to Choose** 35

Inherent Freedom to Choose. Responsibility and Sin. Deliverance from Sin, death, and Law through Christ. Gifts of human Freedoms through Christ. Economic Freedom to Choose inspiration for reconstruction.

3. **The Birth of Jesus Christ for Salvation of the whole human race is stronger than human culture of sin and death** 41

What is salvation through Jesus Christ? The birth of Jesus is announced to the virgin Mary. The virgin Mary's Song of Praise. The birth of Jesus Christ is revealed to Joseph in a dream. The Birth of Jesus. The shepherds and the angels. The visitors from the East. The Words of Simeon. The Word of Life. John the Baptist's Message. The Lamb of God, which takes away the sin of the world.
Why Everyone needs Jesus Christ for Reconstruction and happiness?

4. **The Resurrection of Jesus Christ and Life after Death** 51

The Resurrection of Jesus Christ and the Empty Tomb. Jesus appeared first to the women who went to the Tomb: Mary Magdalene, and Joanna, and Salome, and Mary, the Mother of James. The Report of the Soldiers Guarding the Tomb and the Bribe Money of the Chief Priests. Jesus appeared to his Eleven Disciples and the Apostolic Commission. Unity of the Apostolic Commission and the Farewell Summit Declaration of Jesus Christ: " I am the Way; I am Truth and Life. No one can come to the Father except through me." The Vision of the Last Judgement of Jesus Christ. The Particular Judgement and Life after Death. The Last Judgement and Life after Death.

PART TWO

THE PROFESSION OF THE CHRISTIAN FAITH FOR SELF-RENEWAL

5. **The Profession of the Christian Faith in the Living God through the Most Holy Trinity** 59

What is faith in the invisible living God? Nature of God and of the Most Holy Trinity. The Apostles' Creed. The Nicene Creed. Faith in God is accepting the invitation of God to his Son's wedding Feast. The Farewell Summit Declaration of Jesus Christ: I am the Way; I am Truth and Life. No one can come to the Father except through me." God's Glory in Creation. The Law of the Lord is Perfect.

PART THREE

PRINCIPLES OF MANAGING INDUSTRY TRADE AND COMMERCE FOR REWARD WITH CONFIDENCE IN THE CONTEXT OF INSPIRATION BY THE HOLY SPIRIT

6. **Principles of Managing Industry Trade and Commerce for Reward with Faith in God.** 73

1. What is management? 2. The Lord's parable of the talents is instructive. 3. Faith in the living God is the cause and effect of the goals, vision and value of every human being. 4. Faith in the living

God is the cause and effect of Wisdom for creativity endowed in our soul through Christ. 5. Faith in the living God is the cause and effect of effective communication endowed in our soul through Christ. 6. Faith in the living God is the cause and effect of time management endowed in our soul through Christ. 7. Absence of The New Vision and Self-Renewal Through Faith in Jesus Christ is the cause and effect of stress, which affects our health and life. 8. Faith in the living God is the cause and effect of responsibility and reward endowed in our soul through Christ. 9. Just one thing is needed. 10. According to your faith, let it be unto you.

PART FOUR
HUMAN FREEDOM IN THE SPIRIT OF CHRIST

7. **Human Freedom in the Spirit of Jesus Christ** 81

Preserve your Salvation and Freedom from the Evil One. The Spirit and human nature are enemies. The fruit of human nature. The fruits of the Spirit. Bear one another's Burden. Judge your own Conduct. Do not become tired of Doing Good: Sow and Reap only in the field of the Spirit. 2. No one can say "Jesus is Lord" without being informed by the Holy Spirit. 3. The Love of God and One Another. 4. The Lost Son, who Repented and returned to his Father: Celebration of his Repentance.

8. **The Lord's Sermon on the Mount for Self-Renewal** 88

True Happiness. You are the salt for transforming the whole human race. You are the light for the whole human race. Teaching about the Law and fulfilment of the Law. Teaching about anger: the new standard higher than the old. Teaching about adultery: the new standard higher than the old. Teaching about divorce: the new standard higher than the old. Teaching about vows: the new standard higher than the old. Teaching about revenge: the new standard higher than the old. Love of Enemies: the new standard higher than the old. Teaching about charity: almsgiving in secret. Teaching about Prayer: Prayer in secret. How to pray. The Lord's Prayer. Teaching about fasting: Fasting in secret. Riches in heaven: True treasures. The eye, the lamp of the body. Possessions: Trust only the invisible true God. Do not judge others. Do not profane sacred things. Ask, Seek, Knock: effective Prayer. The golden rule. The narrow and wide gate: Do not follow the crowd but follow only Christ. A tree and its fruit: Know the false prophets by the quality of their life and fruit. Be the true disciple of Christ else I will say to you I never knew you. The true disciple of Christ builds on rock. The false disciple builds on sand. The Authority of Jesus Christ.

9. **The Ten Commandments for Self-Renewal in the context of human rights** 97

The Biblical version of the Ten Commandments. The short version of the Ten Commandments. Application of the Ten Commandments for Self-renewal. Reducing the Ten Commandments into two Commandments based on Love. Who is my neighbour? The parable of the good Samaritan response. What are the human rights in the Ten Commandments for Reconstruction and Happiness?

PART FIVE

PRAYER AND THE GRACE OF THE SACRAMENTS FOR SELF-RENEWAL

10. **Prayer in the Life of the whole human race for Self-Renewal** 105

What is prayer? Adoration. Blessing. Meditation. Contemplation. Vocal prayer. How do we know whether what we are doing is prayer to God? The Christian Liturgy. The Lord's Prayer. The Lord is my shepherd. The Hail Mary. Hail Holy Queen. The Prayer of St Francis of Assisi. Glory be. Prayer for the dead. An Act of love of God and Nieghbour. Prayer is answered in a state of humility and freedom from the world. Warning against Judging another person and a Fellow-Christian. Warning for the Rich and the Over-confident person. The Parable of the Widow and the Judge.

11. **Sacrament of Baptism.** 117

Scriptural source of Baptism in the Holy Spirit of Jesus Christ. What is Baptism? Christian initiation. Basic essentials of Baptism in the Latin Rite. The Baptismal Promises. Essential Elements and Formalities of Baptism. Who can Baptize? Who can receive Baptism? Necessity of Baptism for salvation through Christ. Fruits and grace of Baptism.

12. **Sacrament of Confirmation, Chrismation.** 121

Scriptural source of Confirmation for more activity of the Holy Spirit in the faithful Christian
What is Confirmation? Essential Elements and Formalities of Confirmation. Basic essential rite of Confirmation. Who can give Confirmation? Who can receive Confirmation? Necessity of Confirmation. Fruits and grace of Confirmation.

13. **Sacrament of the Eucharist, Blessed Sacrament, Communion in the context of the Holy Sacrifice of the Mass.** 125

Scriptural source of the Eucharist bread and wine as the living body and blood of Christ. What is the Sacrament of the Eucharist? Basic essentials of the Eucharist celebration in the Roman rite. Essential elements and Formalities of celebrating the Eucharist in the context of the Holy Sacrifice of the Mass in the Roman rite. Who can celebrate the Eucharist? Who can receive the Holy Communion? Necessity of celebrating the Eucharist. Fruits and grace of receiving the Holy Communion.

14. **Sacrament of Confession, Penance, Reconciliation for Healing and Health for Self-Renewal** 133

Scriptural Source of Forgiveness of sin. What is sin? What is Confession of sin? Basic essential rite of Confession. Essential Elements and Formalities of Confession. Who can forgive sin? Who can make confession of sin? Fruits and grace of confession and forgiveness of sin.

15. **Sacrament of Anointing the Sick for Healing and Health** 139

Scriptural source of the Sacrament of Anointing the Sick. What is the sacrament of Anointing the Sick? Basic essential rite of Anointing the Sick. Essential Elements and Formalities of Anointing the Sick. Who can administer the sacrament of Anointing the Sick? Who can receive the sacrament of Anointing the Sick? Fruits and grace of receiving the sacrament of Anointing the Sick.

16. **Sacrament of Marriage and the Family under the Grace of God** 143

Marriage or Matrimony as a Christian Sacrament and Scriptural source. 2. Special Agreement between a man and a woman. 3. With Full Essential rite of Marriage and Matrimonial Consent. 4. The Love of the Spouses requires Unity and Indissolubility of the Marriage. 5. The Love of the Spouses requires Faithfulness of the Spouses to their Marriage Promise of Total Commitment. 6. The Love of the Spouses requires Openness to Fertility, Procreation and Education of Offspring in a Christian Family. 7. Essential Formalities of Sacrament of Marriage. 8. Who can confer Sacrament of Marriage? 9. Who can be a party to the Sacrament of Marriage? 10. Necessity of Sacrament of Marriage. 11. Fruits and grace of Sacrament of Marriage. 12. Sexual activity outside Marriage is a Sin against God and one's Neighbour. 13. Marriage and the Family under the Regime of sin and the Grace of God through Christ.

17. Sacrament of Holy Orders for Renewal of the whole human race **161**

Scriptural Souce of Holy Orders. What is the sacrament of Holy Orders? The institution of the Church and the Mission of the Apostolic Ministry. Basic Essentials of Ordination in the Latin rite. Essential Elements and Formalities of Ordination in the Latin rite. Who can confer Holy Orders in the Latin Rite? Who can receive Holy Orders in the Latin rite? Fruits and grace of Holy Orders.

18. Christian Funeral and Farewell Commendation to God **167**

What is the Christian meaning of Death? What is a Christian Funeral? The Christian Funeral is not a Sacramental. The Greeting of faith of the Community. The Liturgy of the Word. The Eucharistic Sacrifice of the Mass. Farewell Commendation of the Soul of the Deceased to God.

19. The New Vision in the Holy Spirit of Jesus Christ and Self-Renewal Through Faith in Jesus Christ. Use this Book Daily for the Gifts of the Holy Spirit, the Lord, the giver of Life and for Inspiration for Reconstruction **171**

Appendix

1. Human freedom 's Charitable Objects, Activities and Projects 176
2. Basic Facts of 213 States and Countries of the World. 179
3. World Political Map. (Copyright Reproduced by permission of Oxford Cartographers) 186

LIFE IN THE HOLY SPIRIT OF JESUS CHRIST

(THE BOOK FOR LIFE AND INSPIRATION FOR RECONSTRUCTION)

**"Go away from me Satan!
You are an obstacle on my way,
because these thoughts of yours
don't come from God,
but from human nature."
Mat 16: 23**

**JUBILEE A. D. 2000
COMMEMORATIVE EDITION
AMP**

Ave Maria Publishers Limited

LIFE IN THE HOLY SPIRIT OF JESUS CHRIST

(THE BOOK FOR LIFE AND INSPIRATION FOR RECONSTRUCTION)

"Life in the Holy Spirit of Jesus Christ" offers the stable and everlasting infrastructure for promoting the flow of international capital investment worldwide in the context of the revolutionary principles of Christianity in order to arrest poverty and to improve the quality of life worldwide. This everlasting infrastructure gives stability, life, growth and inspiration for reconstruction and happiness to those who understand the principles. Love or truth has no barrier.

This book is addressed to youngsters, students, international capital investors and investees, Christians and non-Christians and the whole international community in order that we can altogether understand the impact of the nature of the God we worship, as an infrastructure of a country, for improving the quality of life worldwide. There is more to life than meets the eye.

Use this book and it will work for you in your own corner. Do not put the cart before the horse.

JUBILEE A. D. 2000
COMMEMORATIVE EDITION
AMP
Ave Maria Publishers Limited

Introduction

"Human beings cannot live on bread alone,
but need every word that God speaks" (Matt 4:4) GNB

Purpose of this book. What is the Christian meaning of Love? The love of Jesus Christ is stronger than human culture of ignorance of God, sin and death. Self-Renewal for Personal Development, Reconstruction and Happiness. Coverage of this book. The Spirit driving the research and publishing of this book in the context of UN policy. Who should use this book. How to use this book. Table of Followers of all Faiths Worldwide.

Purpose of this book

In the name of the Father, and of the Son, and of the Holy Spirit. Amen. Many people are taking an increasing interest in the principles of Christianity as tools for guiding the conduct of people, and for inspiration for reconstruction, and for improving the quality of life worldwide. Indeed, the people of a country are the true investment of the country. This book is an investment of the word of God in the people of any country so that the people can bear much fruit that endures for enjoyment.

According to the Encyclopaedia Britannica, Christianity, the largest of the world's faiths, has a constituency of some two billion believers, out of 5.8 billion of the world population. The people are entitled to empowerment, and equipment and motivation for reconstruction in their own corner of the world. This book is your Companion for life and inspiration for reconstruction.

Let the mind, the tool of observation of the observer, be clean and still.

There is only one stream of truth and love for inspiration for reconstruction. The Christian goal is to know and experience union in the unity of the Most Holy Trinity for inspiration for reconstruction. Know and remember always that you are in the presence of God. This book will help you to know that almighty Omnipresence.

That stillness is the decisive Centre of peace, creativity, reconstruction, health and happiness, and the Kingdom of God or Heaven within you.

It is easier for a camel to go through the eye of a needle than for a rich person to enter the stillness and the Kingdom of God or Heaven.

The first purpose of this book is to help everyone, *through the framework of the Scriptures,* to know the Centre of stillness and silence within, and to sing and dance in it, and to think within for reconstruction in one's corner. Knowledge of that stillness is motivation, empowerment and equipment for reconstruction worldwide. Use this book daily. Practice makes perfect.

Devotion or love through the Holy Spirit of Jesus Christ is the key to revelation and knowledge. Christ never deceives and cannot be deceived by anyone. This book is your Guide and Companion through Christ, the Great Teacher of all seasons.

The second purpose of this book is to offer, *through the framework of the Scriptures,* a harmonious understanding of the Good News of Love from God and salvation for the whole human race through Jesus Christ for self-renewal and inspiration for reconstruction worldwide. This book is for refreshment, for the sinner and the saint, and for clarity of mind, heart, thought, and for clarity of decision-making in private and public life.

God's instruction to Christ Jesus is to free the whole human race from human culture of servitude to ignorance, sin and death. The love of Jesus Christ for renewal and inspiration of the whole human race for reconstruction is stronger than human culture of ignorance, sin and death. Reconstruction is possible only through that Christian freedom, which destroyed ignorance for good.

Ignorance of God is the fundamental barrier to inspiration for reconstruction and the flow of international capital investment. Reconstruction is interior and external conversion and for improving the quality of life of the whole human race.

Feed your mind for reconstruction through life in the Holy Spirit of Jesus Christ. Your mind is your instrument for observing the details of knowledge for reconstruction. Persistent use of this book will help you in your observation of the details. Follow and practise the teachings of Jesus Christ in this book.

People have plenty of food to eat in Europe and North America, yet some of them are hungry. People have plenty of food to eat in Africa, Asia, America, Europe and the rest of the world, yet some of them are starving. People take holidays from work in order to have a rest; yet they cry for more rest. People are in bed to sleep; but they cannot sleep. People make wrong decisions because their decisions are based on human nature. People use drugs, like cannabis, cocaine, opium and heroin for satisfaction, yet they are not satisfied. People go on diet to get slim and healthy, yet it makes no difference. Why is it so? It is so because "Human beings cannot live on bread alone, but need every word that God speaks".(Matt 4:4).This book will help you to know the difference.

The word of God is powerful to break down every limitation of the human being. The word of God enables anyone to expand with ability to think and take decisions in the context of the thoughts and decisions of God and achieve anything through Jesus Christ. Practice makes perfect.

Living on bread alone is idolatry. Idolatry is worshipping the creation instead of the Creator. There is only one Word and one God. The Most Holy Trinity is one indivisible God in three persons: Father, and the Son, and the Holy Spirit; and each of the three persons is God *whole, entire and perfect.*

Feed your mind with the word that God speaks and you cannot be hungry. Feed your mind with the word that God speaks and you cannot be starving. Feed your mind with the word that God speaks and you will be healthy and happy. Adopt the decision, which God had made and you cannot be a wrong decision-maker. There is a place for a rest in the word that God speaks; you cannot be restless. This book offers the word that God speaks to enable you to eat to live, to feed your mind for reconstruction, and have a true rest in the love of God and Jesus Christ for the whole human race.

There is more to life than the gross domestic product (G D P) of a country or productivity. This means human beings cannot live on bread alone, but every word of God in this book. This means transparency in private and public life and obeying the rules of conduct of Jesus Christ, the King, the Prophet and the Judge. This book will take you through the new rules, which changed the old rules of the Ten Commandments.

There is more to life than meets the eye. That invisible "more" is "Life in the Holy Spirit of Jesus Christ". That life is the everlasting and transcendent reality and love. That life is freedom from human culture of servitude to sin and death. In that freedom, the invisible reveals itself for personal development and reconstruction worldwide. The invisible is Love. Love is constructive.

This book is "Life in the Holy Spirit of Jesus Christ." This book is also called "The Book for Life and Inspiration for Reconstruction" because of its source in the Holy Spirit, the Lord, the giver of life. The Holy Spirit is the source of all inspiration. The Holy Spirit generates inspiration. Inspiration means information. Inspiration generates discipline. The purpose of inspiration is for reconstruction.

You are not an island. Be connected always to the Holy Spirit of Jesus Christ within you. The Holy Spirit has an abode in you; it has a house within you. You can enter this house and take out any grace and glory of God for your use and enjoyment. Devotion is the key to this inner temple within you.

You will receive inspiration, and the grace and glory of God by complying with the commands and teachings of Jesus Christ in this book. More compliance means more inspiration. Inspiration is the foundation stone for stability and reconstruction worldwide.

The third purpose is to offer the love of Jesus Christ for the whole human race, *through the framework of the Scriptures,* for *education of every one* and for *controlling one's human nature.* Self-control of the human nature enables personal development and inspiration for reconstruction; it enables one to reduce the strain and stress of life and to increase longevity and happiness of life.

Human nature is opposed to the nature of God. God is Love. Love is creative. Every enduring decision must be taken independent of human nature. This means the mind, which is the instrument of decision-making, must be *detached from human nature and attached only to the nature of God.*

Human nature is a matter of form according to human judgement. The many forms of human nature include one's name, address, house, nationality, body, bones, height, colour, size, sex, possessions, money, power, status, rank, citizenship and so on. These are not our true nature. But they are important and should be properly used. People boast about them. But boasting is a form of human nature. Our true nature is divine, inspiring and constructive.

People think happiness depends on the country in which one lives or one's nationality. This is not true. There are happy and unhappy people in every country in the world. Some countries have better infrastructure and this is an advantage for improving the quality of life. Infrastructure includes things like hospitals, nursing homes, convalescent homes, schools, educational institutions, technology, communication by air, road and sea, computer literates, accountants, management consultants, banks, the nature of God one worships, and law and order. Human nature is attached to all these infrastructures. Happiness depends on how one thinks within and not on a country's infrastructure. This book is your guide to full life and happiness.

Human freedom means freedom from servitude to ignorance, sin and death. Freedom means Christian life, which is independent of human nature and dependent on the nature of God only.

The fourth purpose is to offer, *through the framework of the Scriptures,* the culture of "*Life in the Holy Spirit of Jesus Christ,*" for in-depth prayer and evangelisation of the whole human race in the context of the culture of the people. Evangelisation means spreading the Good News of Jesus Christ for improving the quality of life.

Prayer is thinking the thoughts of God and not the thoughts of human beings. Prayer is making our own the decisions, which God had already made for the whole human race and not making our own human decisions based on our human nature.

The fifth purpose is to help everyone to say daily private prayer to God *through the framework of the Scriptures* for renewal of faith, hope and the love of God and one another, and for personal development and transformation, and for deepening the spiritual life of everyone. This transformation will enable everyone to go into the world for reconstruction and bear much fruit that endures.

In order to bear much fruit that endures, one must not focus on the history and past events or worry about tomorrow but focus on the issues of the day and one can provide for today and tomorrow. There is no need to add to the troubles each day brings.

The sixth purpose is to help everyone *to pray effectively through the framework of the Scriptures,* in order to lead the whole human race to the only freedom and love on earth as in heaven. Thus, everyone will know the Way to the Father, the Truth and the Life. This book is the pilgrim's Companion.

The seventh and final purpose is to help everyone to reply to God for his grace and love for the whole human race, and to integrate the love of God into our daily life, and to have reconciliation with God, and to share in the glory and happiness of God through Christ. This book is your guide.

Christ Jesus brings the message of love for reconstruction, personal development and happiness. He brings a story of love. He brings a message of love from God. Love comes from God, the Father of our Lord Jesus Christ, and our Father in heaven. God is Spirit. Understanding the love of Christ for the human race helps everyone to understand how important one is in the eye of God.

God is love. Love comes from God through Christ. Love draws together in union all things that are different. Love is the only principle of revolution, which is radical, transparent and can be trusted by the whole human race to transform the world for Christ against the forces of sin and death. The love of God and one another, as Christ loves us, is the only means, which justifies the meaning of life.

The love of God for the whole human race through Christ is stronger than human culture of servitude to ignorance, sin and death. Human culture of servitude to ignorance, sin and death against God can be overcome through life in the Holy Spirit of Jesus Christ.

God wants the whole human race to reply to his story of love as he truly is with all our strength and talents through life in the Holy Spirit of Jesus Christ. This book offers a summary of the love story brought by Christ and how to reply to him. You will know what is the meaning of love, not according to the meaning of the world, but according to the meaning of Christ Jesus.

Overall, this book is based on the love revolution of Jesus Christ, *through the Scriptures,* for constructive personal development and inspiration for reconstruction. It is not a biography of the author but a sharing of the love of God for the whole human race, through "*Life in the Holy Spirit of Jesus Christ*". Its message transcends every denominational, religious, political and national boundary. In this context, this book is addressed to students, youngsters and people worldwide for inspiration for reconstruction in their own corner.

The theme is life and inspiration for reconstruction and happiness through Jesus Christ worldwide. He is ever faithful, loving, happy, inspiring, constructive and true to his name. The Father reveals and fulfils himself through him and he reveals the Father to the whole human race. God became a human being and dwelt among us. So that human beings may become inspired and be constructive.

What is the Christian meaning of Love?

"My commandment is this: love one another just as I love you." (Jn 15: 12)

"Love one another just as I love you." is the summary of the whole love story of God for the whole human race brought by Jesus Christ. But what does Jesus Christ mean by the word "love"? Here are ten elements of the love of God for the whole human race and the love of one another.

1. *Love is accepting people as part of oneself, body and family.* Everyone is your brother and sister. There should be no discrimination on ground of language, tribe, sex, race, colour, status, rank, religion, politics, culture, class or age. All made in the image and likeness of God. Get into union with people through Christ. *Transform* people and their quality of life. Play the Good Samaritan with all your resources.
2. *Love is replying to God by opening oneself to people.* It is as if God has written a love letter to you. Open the letter quick and read it. Meditate on the message with all your soul, mind, heart and strength. You have to reply it prompt. Do not shut up yourself in a shell like an oyster. Be caring for others. See people as they are. Don't be blind. Take the other person into account. Look out for people. Look for them. Go to meet them. Be kind to them. Give out all you have to them. Don't see only yourself.

Tolerate people as they are. Put on people as you put on Christ. Educate people to come to their senses and to return to their father as the lost son did.

3. *Love is helping people to fulfil their full potential life.* Dedicate yourself to help people and not only yourself. Help to transform people. Help them to become holy like God. Help people to fulfil their hope and expectations. Help them have faith in God. Help them to change their false beliefs and culture. Educate them in the love of God for the whole human race. Be a mentor to people. Teach them the skill of your trade, profession, vocation and employment so that we can all share in the glory of God.
4. *Love of God for the whole human race is unconditional and it is stronger than human culture of sin and death.* The people are not worthy of the love and forgiveness of God. The people can not give consideration for the love and forgiveness of God. They cannot make down payment for the love and forgiveness of God. They cannot make up-front payment for the love and forgiveness of God. God himself makes the down payment and the up-front payment by his love and mercy. God forgives. Love forgives and carries away the sin of the world. We are forgiven before our repentance. What amazing love! *The love of God is stronger than human culture of sin and death.* The free gift of love of Jesus Christ for the whole human race is powerful enough to banish poverty in the world. That gift of love must be accepted by the whole human race before poverty can be banished every where.
5. *Love is playing Martha and Mary and not to become absorbed exclusively with Martha or Mary.* Harmonise and integrate your temporary and worldly interests with your interests in the love of God and people.
6. *Love renews people through Christ.* Love seeks to make people holy just as God is holy. No one can enter the Kingdom of God without being born again of water and the Holy Spirit of Christ. You must be born again.
7. *There is only one love, which embraces God and the whole human*

race. God is invisible. A person who cannot love his sister or brother that one can see cannot claim to love God, whom one has never seen. Love of the person you can see is the love of God. That love is our only heritage.

8. *Love is creative and it transforms the world.* Love can change the past through Christ. Love can liberate people from the burden of their culture and false human thought of the past for a new creative start. We owe our civilisation to the love of God. Love is constructive.

   In a land or country without love, there is no development and reconstruction. The decision-makers seek only things of this world for themselves. They see only themselves and not the people as a whole. They are blind and dead. Love improves the quality of life of people as a whole.

9. *Love is Christ Jesus and his way of life.* Love is begotten and not made. Love is the message. Love is the messenger. The messenger is God. God is love. The person who loves must be born again in the Holy Spirit of Christ.

   Love transforms people and their quality of life. Christ sets the standard of love and not the world. Love people as Christ loves people. Love is sharing the glory of God with people.

   Love draws together like a magnet all who are *different* in size, shape, colour, race, status, culture and belief without any discrimination. Love transforms the world below and above. Love lasts forever.

   Love is Christ Jesus, who is a "person," always alive and present with us. Love is knowing Jesus Christ as he knows the whole human race. Love has inner strength and is brave and courageous. Love never gives up.

   Jesus Christ came into the world to forgive sin. *The love of Christ for the whole human race is stronger than sin and death. The love of Christ is stronger than human culture of sin and death.* Even the horrible sin of Saint Paul of persecuting the early Christians before his dramatic conversion was forgiven. That is the Good News of God's love for the whole human race. *That is the faith of the Church.*

That Good News of love is what all Christians must proclaim in their heart and carry to every corner of the world. Love is a world without end. Everything shall pass away with our earthly pilgrimage. The whole beautiful world in which we live and move shall pass away. But love shall not pass away; love is a world without end.

Love never passes away. Love is the foundation and the only content of everlasting life. Faith, hope and love are the three things that last. Of these three, the greatest is love. (1 Cor.13:13) Jesus is that model of love.

10. *The true meaning of love is life in the Holy Spirit of Jesus Christ on earth, which leads to God in heaven.* There is a place, a house, a mansion, a palace and a home in the love of God for the whole human race.

Wherever love is, human rights are respected by all. Love is the vision of the Particular and Last Judgement of Jesus Christ.

The love of Jesus Christ is stronger than human culture of sin and death

Thanksgiving worship for our salvation through Jesus Christ, prayer, faith, hope and the love of God and our brothers and sisters as Christ loves us, and evangelisation are the central agenda of life in the Holy Spirit of Jesus Christ for reconstruction and happiness. Of these the greatest is the love of God and our brothers and sisters as Christ loves us. The love of Jesus Christ for the whole human race is stronger than human culture of sin and death.

Prayer is thinking God's thought and making it one's own; listening to God, making the decisions God makes, doing the will of God on earth as in heaven, and experiencing the love of God through Christ.

Prayer begins from the beginning of the creation and ends with the end of the creation. The Scriptures offer the divine models and framework of prayer and within that framework everyone should be able to pray and listen through Christ.

Prayer must be in harmony with the prayer and the will of God; it must be in harmony with the prayer of our Lord Jesus Christ. Anything short of that glory is an opposition to God, and to Christ, and to the Holy Spirit, and it will not be heard nor answered.

Our Lord's Prayer, the Hail Mary, the Hail Holy Queen, Our Lord's Sermon on the Mount, the Ten Commandments, the salvation message of Christ to the whole human race, our Lord's dialogue with his disciples in preparation for his death and his prayer for his disciples and the faithful before his death and resurrection, the sacramental mandate of Christ for ministry in his Church, and indeed the Scriptures of the Holy Bible offer divine frameworks and models of prayer for everyone. The Creator inscribed the nature of prayer to the living God of love in the heart, soul and spirit of everyone. Hence the everlasting search to discover God in the heart.

Ignorance of the love of God for the whole human race and of the way to God is a concession to human weakness since the Fall of the first man and woman created by God. Our Lord Jesus Christ, our Saviour, firmly responds: "I am the Way; I am Truth and Life. No one can come to the Father except through me." John 14: 6 JB. He is the Way, the Truth and the Life because he is love.

Your prayers and soul cannot be accepted in the Kingdom of God unless they are in harmony with the divine plan, will and prayer. They must be in harmony with the Way, the Truth and the Life of our Lord Jesus Christ.

In the beginning the creation was bliss. The purpose of the creation is to fulfil the will of the Creator on earth as in heaven. The purpose is to satisfy what the Spirit needs and not to satisfy human nature.

Human disobedience of the Creator led to the first sin against God, the original sin, and the consequential disorder in human nature. Human nature became imperfect. Harmony with the Creator was broken because man and woman were driven by the Evil One to act not in the Spirit of Christ but according to what human nature tells them to do. However, the love of God for the whole human race is stronger than human servitude to sin and death.

God fulfilled himself again through his Son, Jesus Christ. The Son, who was at the side of the Father at the time of the creation of heaven and earth, was sent by the Father to save and free the whole human race from sin and the power of the Evil One. Further, to offer forgiveness of God for human disobedience and sin and reconciliation with God, our Father in heaven. This is salvation by God through Christ. Salvation means redemption of the whole human race by Christ from the power of the Evil One to the everlasting life of God. Once again the love of Jesus Christ for the whole human race is stronger than human error and sin.

Jesus Christ, our only Saviour under the Sun, did carry out his salvation mission. Through Christ, the Father reveals himself, his Son and his Holy Spirit to the whole human race. Christ carried out the will of his Father and is now seated at the right hand of God, our Father in heaven.

After the salvation works of Jesus Christ, it is the personal responsibility of every person to accept salvation and forgiveness of our sin by God through Christ. Responsibility means we must pray and love God and one another in the Spirit of Christ in order to resist falling again into the power and temptation of the Evil One. We can because the love of God is stronger than every temptation and sin.

Thus, the book is a retreat for everyone for salvation and forgiveness of sins by God through our Saviour Jesus Christ and reconciliation with God. The book offers refreshment in the Holy Spirit of Christ for self-renewal, healing, health and fitness for the spiritual journey and worship of only the living God and not the creation.

Life in the Holy Spirit of Christ is an experience of the presence and the love of God. That life breaks down every barrier to salvation within and without. That life enables works for the improvement of the quality of life of the people of God worldwide. Prayerful meditation with this book will help you to experience life in the Holy Spirit of Christ and the presence of Christ. God is Spirit and can only be experienced by his own gift to the faithful. Faith is a gift of God.

"We know that in all things God works for good with those who love him, those whom he has called according to his purpose. Those whom God had already chosen he also set apart to become like his Son, so that the Son would be the eldest brother in a large family. And to those whom God set apart, he called; and those he called, he put right with himself, and he shared his glory with them." (Rom 8: 28-30)

This private prayer and meditation book is educational for life. God helps those who help themselves. This book can help you to know yourself, free yourself from doing what human nature wants you to do, heal yourself, deepen your faith in God and in Jesus Christ, renew your soul, change your vision for good, practise life in the Spirit of Christ, know where you are going, know how God thinks and makes decisions through Christ for you, for every genius and for the whole human race, pray effectively through the Scriptures, manage your thoughts, actions, responsibilities, emotions, talents and fulfil your goals in union with Christ, share in the glory of God and improve the quality of your life.

This is the book for life and inspiration for reconstruction worldwide.

Self-Renewal for Personal Development, Reconstruction and Happiness

Self-renewal is the wisdom of making holy one's physical, mental, emotional and spiritual nature in union with Christ. Self-renewal enables one to find more energy, light, unconditional love and the gifts of the Holy Spirit in order to respond effectively to one's goals, vision and responsibilities. Self-renewal enables one to limit or take away the damage of sin to one's life and to receive the grace of God through Christ. Self-renewal enables everyone to stop to consider on the world stage one's goals, vision and responsibilities in any trade, profession, vocation, employment and family in union with Christ in order to know the difference.

Self-renewal is wisdom of necessity not only for the whole human race but for God through Jesus Christ. Self-renewal leads to self-knowledge and enlightenment. In a state of self-renewal, one will freely choose and act on one's own value driven goals and one will not be acted upon by others.

Self-knowledge is the recognition of the abilities of one to freely think, to determine or choose one's own value-driven goals and responsibilities in any trade, profession, vocation, employment or family in union with Christ. The truth shall set you free from the errors of the ages to enable you to determine your own goals and freely respond or choose your responsibilities through Christ.

Self-knowledge is promoted through education and training of the human conscience, imagination, self-determination and the will power to act. These inherent powers are endowed in every human being through Christ.

Conscience enables one to know what is good or evil and it enables one to freely choose what is good for one and others and to reject what is evil. Conscience is able to choose or respond effectively to one's responsibilities only when it is educated, trained and well formed.

The Christian faith, as illustrated in the Lord's parable of the talents, is an invaluable grace of God for self-renewal and self-knowledge endowed in the soul of every human being through Jesus Christ. The Christian faith and the whole creation are invaluable assets entrusted to the whole human race by God through Christ, whom God sent to the whole human race. Jesus Christ is Light from Light for the whole human race, God from God, true God from true God, the Son of the living God.

Management means using certain skills or tools to make things happen in order to meet the value driven goals of any enterprise in union with the Christ in you. This means one must focus on one's own value driven responsibilities in a state of self-renewal in union with Christ.

In the new state of self-renewal, one receives the gift of the Holy Spirit. The Holy Spirit teaches one self-management and development in any trade, profession, vocation, employment and family through Christ.

In a state of self-renewal, one is aware that everything is transparent; everybody is living in a glass house; nothing is hidden and one acts with integrity and truth in every relationship. In a state of true self-renewal anything one touches turns into gold by virtue of the truth and the light underlying one's transactions and relationship with others.

The Holy Spirit teaches the user of this book to know the true meaning of self-renewal for personal management and development and to share in that rich heritage and glory of God through faith in the risen Lord Jesus Christ.

You can achieve that goal because Christ is in you and you are in Christ. Any one who is in Christ is a new person through Christ and he or she can share in the glory of God.

"God's plan is to make known his secret to his people, this rich and glorious secret which he has for all peoples. And the secret is that Christ is in you, which means that you will share in the glory of God." Col 1: 27. "For the full content of divine nature lives in Christ, in his humanity, and you have been given full life in union with him. He is supreme over every spiritual ruler and authority." *Col 2: 9-10.*

Someone may ask how can I share in the glory of God? The Christ in you will do his own works and not you. Christ keeps his promise and commitment. Christ never deceives and cannot be deceived by anyone.

"I am telling you the truth: those who believe in me will do what I do – yes, they will do even greater things, because I am going to the Father. And I will do whatever you ask for in my name, so that the Father's glory will be shown through the Son. If you ask me for anything in my name, I will do it." *Jn. 14: 12-14.*

The new Law and Order has come through Christ. That means all our sins are carried away through the great Sacrifice of Christ, who died for us on the Cross and Resurrected. Christ has forgiven the sin of the whole human race since Adam and Eve. We are restored to the favour of God through the merit of Christ. We are friends of God through Christ. Christ has freed the whole human race from the Evil One. Christ has destroyed the fear of death and every form of fear and limitation of the Evil One.

Some one may ask how the Scriptures fit into personal management and development in the context of the Lord's parable of the talents in a world economy based on the survival of the fittest at home and abroad?

"All Scripture is inspired by God and is useful for teaching the truth, rebuking error, correcting faults, and giving instruction for right living, so that the person who serves God may be fully qualified and equipped to do every kind of good deed." *2 Tim 3: 16-17.*

This book is your tool for self-renewal to enable you to evaluate your goals and vision in any trade, profession, vocation, employment and family on the world stage in union with Christ. This book is written to help and guide you to achieve your goal in this world and eternal life through Christ.

"And eternal life means knowing you, the only true God, and knowing Jesus Christ, whom you sent." *Jn 17: 3.*

Coverage of this book

Life in the Holy Spirit of Jesus Christ presents, *through the framework of the Scriptures,* a harmonious understanding of the Good News of Love from God and salvation for the whole human race through Jesus Christ for personal development and inspiration for reconstruction worldwide. God's instruction to Christ Jesus is to liberate the whole human race from human culture of servitude to sin and death.

The love of God and Jesus Christ for reconstruction and happiness worldwide is stronger than human culture of servitude to sin and death. Love is creative. Love is inventive. Love is constructive. Love renews the world through Christ.

This book has the following twelve features:-

1. It is a book for life and inspiration for reconstruction and happiness worldwide. There is more to life than meets the eye.
2. It promotes personal development and business management with

integrity in the context of the Spiritual principle of love taught by Jesus Christ. Thus, love creates, constructs, and develops anything. Love renews the world. Knowledge is power.

3. It can help one to market and sell any service and product with integrity by applying to whatever one is doing the principles of love taught by Jesus Christ.
4. It is educational on the moral principles of the right conduct in public and private life, based on love, which is respectable by the whole human race and which should be applied to the management of any trade, profession, vocation and employment worldwide.
5. It is inspiring and uplifting from darkness and groom to light for improvement in one's quality of life.
6. It promotes personal health and healing and helps one to control stress and longevity of life.
7. It helps one to control every fear and in particular the fear of death.
8. It helps one to get the courage and confidence to act, to create, to develop, to construct, to apply effectively one's inherent talent and invest in people worldwide. Understand that the goal of the heritage is to invest in people.
9. It helps one to be free from living in servitude to sin and death. The love of Jesus Christ, who died for us, is stronger than human culture of servitude to sin and death.
10. It helps one to understand human nature and the nature of God; and helps one to avoid doing what human nature and human greed tells one to do and obey only the commands of Jesus Christ.
11. It helps one to have tranquillity and a true rest and happiness in the love of God and Jesus Christ for the whole human race. In that state, God will reveal itself and glory to you, guide you and teach you everything about the way of God and life.
12. It helps one to experience the love of God for the whole human race and to have the true freedom to choose, to invest in people and to enjoy life and the glory of God and Jesus Christ in its fullness.

The love of God and salvation message of Christ still resonates in our hearts after two thousand years. The message is for the renewal of the whole human race, through life in the Holy Spirit of Christ. Jesus Christ brings the message of love and happiness for reconstruction of the world. "And now I make all things new!" (Rev 21: 5) The love of Jesus Christ for the whole human race is stronger than human culture of sin and death.

The content of this book is divided into five interrelated parts as follows. *Freedom to choose everlasting life in the Holy Spirit of Christ or human culture of servitude to sin and death. *The profession of the Christian faith for self-renewal through the Most Holy Trinity, the invisible one God in three persons. *The principles of managing industry, trade and commerce for reward with confidence in the context of the parable of the talents. *Life in the Holy Spirit of Christ in the context of the Lord's Sermon on the Mount and the Ten Commandments. *Nature of prayer and the seven sacraments of the Catholic Church, the Body of Christ. All roads lead to human freedom from servitude to sin and death culture to enable personal development and reconstruction worldwide.

The coverage begins from the creation of man and woman and ends in the everlasting life of God and it includes:-* creation of man and woman and the first family. *The quest for happiness and self-knowledge. *Human ability to respond to God with the talents invested in our soul by God for reward through Christ. *Human freedom to choose everlasting life in the Spirit of Christ or death. *Responsibility and human disobedience and the original sin and suffering of the whole human race. *Salvation of the whole human race through the Incarnation of Jesus Christ. *Why everyone needs Christ Jesus *The Resurrection of Jesus Christ and life after life for the whole human race. *The Particular and Last Judgement. *The profession of the Christian faith in the name of the Father, and of the Son, and of the Holy Spirit for the renewal of the whole human race. *Nature of God and of the Most Holy Trinity. *The Farewell Summit Declaration of Christ: "I am the Way; I am Truth and Life. No one can come to the Father except through me." *The parable of the talents of Jesus Christ and the principles of managing private enterprise for reward in any trade, profession, vocation and employment with faith in God worldwide. *Life in the Holy Spirit of Christ in contrast with life as dictated by our human nature. *Our Lord's Sermon on the Mount. *The Ten Commandments. What are the human rights in the Ten Commandments? *The nature and skill of daily prayer and meditation with the Scriptures on the will of God to be done on earth as in heaven and to enable the user of this book to encounter the living God of love, compassion, forgiveness and the source of all supplies. *Baptism. *Confirmation. *The Eucharist Communion. *Reconciliation. *Anointing the Sick. *Marriage and the family and the responsibilities of the spouses. *Sexual activity outside Marriage is a sin against God. *Holy Orders. *Christian funeral and life after death. *The new vision of life in the Holy Spirit of Christ and self-renewal through faith in God and in Jesus Christ.

This book is also called "The Book for Life and Inspiration for Reconstruction." This book is inspirational, uplifting, proactive, principle-based, morally and spiritually educational in the love of God for the whole human race and for one another for personal development and reconstruction. This book *offers the love revolution of Jesus Christ for personal development and reconstruction in every country of the world. It offers the everlasting word of the love of God for the whole human race and of one another for personal development and for improving the quality of life of the whole human race.*

Praying and meditating with this book will help you to invite the Holy Spirit of Jesus Christ to stay with you forever, to guide you, and teach you everything, and in particular how to set aside human culture of sin and death for personal growth and development. *The love of God for the whole human race is stronger than human culture of sin and death.*

The love of God for the whole human race heals. Use this book daily to heal yourself in the name of Jesus Christ, the healer of all seasons. Lord, I am not worthy to receive you. But only say the word and I shall be healed. Any one with faith in Jesus Christ will be healed through daily prayer with this book.

Use this book daily for a healthy performance, personal happiness and development. Have a true rest and happiness in the love of God for the whole human race through Jesus Christ.

Human culture of servitude to sin and death is the fundamental cause of poverty, denial of human rights and the fundamental freedoms and unhappiness worldwide. This book will help to liberate the whole human race from human culture of servitude to sin and death and to renew confidence in entrepreneurial culture for reconstruction and development and for improving the quality of life worldwide.

This is "The Book for Life and Inspiration for Reconstruction." The right to life is your inherent human right. Use this book and it will work for you.

The Spirit driving the research and the publishing of this book in the context of UN policy.

This book is the result of the author's interdisciplinary Ph.D study and research on international money investment and development in the London School of Economics and Political Science in the Faculty of Law of the University of London.

This research was driven by the author's desire to know the response of international money investment to life, personal happiness and reconstruction worldwide in the context of the socio-economic policy of UN. The immediate post World War II policy of the UN was to arrest and alleviate poverty, to maintain peace and security and to promote human rights and the fundamental freedoms worldwide. *In truth, to bring to an end human culture of servitude to sin and death against God and one another in every country, state and nation for reconstruction and enjoyment worldwide*

The UN promotes its economic and social policy, through the Economic and Social Council, by promoting and encouraging " (a) higher standards of living, full employment, and conditions of economic and social progress and development; (b) solutions of international economic, social, health, and related problems; and international cultural and educational co-operation; and (c) universal respect for and observance of, human rights and fundamental freedoms for all without distinction as to race, sex, language, or religion." [sub-paragraphs a, b, and c of Article 55 of UN Charter]; [Art 1.3 UN Charter]

This UN policy was promoted through regional economic and social co-operation of member states. The approach was to strengthen economic relations among the regional members themselves and with other outsider countries, in particular in the fields of trade, production, industry, agriculture, transport, housing, building and planning, monetary co-operation, infrastructure, institutional development and development management.

In this wake, five UN Regional Economic Commissions were created. The first was the Economic Commission for Europe (ECE) in 1947, based at Geneva, Switzerland, with 54 member countries in Europe and North America including Israel. The second was Economic and Social Commission for Asia and the Pacific (ESCAP) in 1947, based at Bangkok, Thailand with 48 members and 10 associates. ESCAP represents about sixty percent of the world population, currently estimated at 5.8 billion with increment exceeding 80 million per year. The third was the Economic Commission for Latin America and the Caribbean (ECLAC) in 1948, based at Santiago, Chile with 41 member states and 5 associates. The fourth was Economic Commission for Africa (ECA) in 1958, based at Addis Ababa, Ethiopia with 52 member countries. The fifth was Economic and Social Commission for Western Asia (ESCWA) in 1973, based at Beirut, Lebanon with 13 member states.

At the centre of the five regional Commissions is the UN itself. The UN stands for world peace and security, and respect for universal human rights and fundamental freedoms, and international economic and social co-operation in solving international conflicts. The UN is like a lion in the jungle and its voice is respected by all animals, big or small, in the big and small tribes worldwide. The UN is like a shield from God for the protection of the whole human race without distinction as to language, tribe, sex, race, colour, status, rank, religion, politics, culture, class, or age.

The mandates of the regional Commissions are clear. All of them function within the UN budget. What were found basically missing in the international money investment equation were freedom to choose one's own goal, vision and controlling of one's human nature and responsibilities. The goal of the investment was in fundamental conflict with Article 55 of the UN Charter.

In brief, political and trade, industry and commercial leadership were lacking in many countries of the world. There was nobody or team to answer the question as to who should bell the cat, why, how, when and where?

Indeed, the cart was put before the horse. The inspiring confidence was lost and must be recovered. The entrepreneurial culture needs self-renewal through the love revolution of Jesus Christ for reconstruction and enjoyment worldwide. There is more to life than meets the eye.

Human culture of servitude to sin and death against God and one another is the fundamental cause of the epidemic the UN seeks to arrest and eradicate. The only eternal content of the Universe, in which we live and move, is love. Thus, our Lord Jesus Christ warned the whole human race in his farewell message, "Love one another as I love you."

This book offers a fundamental and a supplementary solution to the post World War II international money investment policy as a tool for improving the quality of life worldwide. Firstly, there should be education of all the players on controlling one's human nature and on the love of God, through Christ, for the whole human race and the love of one another. Thus, human culture of servitude to sin and death against God and one another can be arrested for good. This book offers that education for the whole human race for personal development and reconstruction worldwide.

Secondly, international charitable organisations should adopt constructive fundraising for investment in people in association with private or public companies in order to hasten improvement of the quality of life of the whole human race.

This is an independent, self-help and voluntary programme, which is called Human freedom Plan. The Human freedom Plan is like the Marshall Plan (1948-52) designed to rehabilitate the economies of the post-World War II European nations, in order to create stable conditions in which human freedom and free institutions could flourish. The Marshall Plan was sponsored and financed by the United States alone.

Unlike the Marshall Plan, the Human freedom Plan is an independent, self-help and worldwide programme financed not by one state but by voluntary contributions and participation worldwide. Thus, the whole human race must go forward together and bear much fruit that will endure in stable conditions in which human freedom and independent free institutions could flourish together with the sovereign state. Our Lord's parable of the talents is instructive.

Human Freedom, registered in England, charity No. 1049216, is one of these international charitable and self-help organisations, working under the Human freedom Plan. Human freedom means freedom from human culture of servitude to sin and death.

Ave Maria Publishers Limited (AMP) registered in England No. 4002569 is one of these private companies collaborating with Human freedom for investment in people worldwide under the Human freedom Plan.

Who should use this book?

This book is written for use of any member of the international community in any trade, profession, vocation, employment and family worldwide for self-renewal in order to preserve one's freedom through Christ and to enable the whole human race to see the new vision and to embrace it. Thus, the book is addressed to both Christians of any denomination and non-Christians because its message transcends every culture.

This book should be used by directors, executives, managers, employees and self-employed persons and individuals in any family worldwide to enable all to share in the glory of God through Christ. Through Christ, everything is possible without any limitation.

Recommend the use of this book to members of your family, staff, and your colleagues and friends at home and abroad so that we can all share in the glory of God through Christ.

How to use this book

This book is a daily companion to be used daily to enable the user to enjoy the wisdom of self-renewal and true freedom from the Evil One in union with Christ.

It is an effective reference book for self-renewal in any trade, profession, vocation, employment and family worldwide to enable one to respond proactively to any situation.

"Be sure that the book of the Law is always read in your worship. Study it day and night, and make sure that you obey everything written in it. Then you will be prosperous and successful. Remember that I have commanded you to be determined and confident! Don't be afraid or discouraged, for I, the LORD your God, am with you wherever you go." *Joshua 1: 8-9.*

Use this book faithfully and it will help you to renew yourself, to clarify your purpose in life, your goal, your vision, your values, your responsibilities and your priorities. You will be able to manage yourself, your responsibilities and your relations with others with confidence and your freedom without any stress or hindrance in union with Christ.

Use this book to help you to improve your personal development and management in any trade, profession, vocation, employment and family in union with Christ. Let in the Holy Spirit to help you to solve the problem and to overcome the daily stress. To God everything is possible.

"Do not restrain the Holy Spirit; do not despise inspired messages. Put all things to the test: keep what is good and avoid every kind of evil." *1 Thess: 19-21.*

"Finally, build up your strength in union with the Lord and by means of his mighty power. Put on all the armour that God gives you, so that you will be able to stand up against the Devil's evil tricks. For we are not fighting against human beings but against the wicked spiritual forces in the heavenly world, the rulers, authorities, and cosmic powers of this dark age. So put on God's armour now! Then when the evil day comes, you will be able to resist the enemy's attacks; and after fighting to the end, you will still hold your ground.

"So stand ready, with truth as a belt tight round your waist, with righteousness as your breastplate, and as your shoes the readiness to announce the Good News of peace. At all times carry faith as a shield; for with it you will be able to put out all the burning arrows shot by the Evil One. And accept salvation as a helmet, and the word of God as the sword which the Spirit gives you. Do all this in prayer, asking for God's help. Pray on every occasion, as the Spirit leads. For this reason keep alert and never give up; pray always for all God's people." *Eph 6:10-18.*

"Everyone who wants to live a godly life in union with Christ Jesus will be persecuted; and evil persons and impostors will keep on going from bad to worse, deceiving others and being deceived themselves. But as for you, continue in the truths that you were taught and firmly believe. You know who your teachers were, and you remember that ever since you were a child, you have known the Holy Scriptures, which are able to give you the wisdom that leads to salvation through faith in Christ Jesus." *2 Tim 3: 12-15.*

For all who make themselves great will be humbled, and all who humble themselves will be made great. Christianity is living in a state of self-renewal whereby one is always informed or inspired by the Holy Spirit.

Through him, with him, in him, in the unity of the Holy Spirit, all glory and honour is yours, almighty Father, for ever and ever. Amen.

Table of Followers of all Faiths Worldwide

	Africa	Asia	Europe	Latin America	North America
Christians	**341,208,000**	**300,383,000**	**409,653,000**	**443,056,000**	**241,147,000**
Roman Catholics	128,167,000	130, 102,000	260,034,000	412,366,000	97,992,000
Protestants	91,070,000	85,764,000	73,206,000	17,550,000	97,176,000
Orthodox	29,771,000	3,847,000	35,777,000	1,793,000	6,062,000
Anglicans	28,013,000	744,000	32,629,000	1,322,000	7,404,000
Other Christians	64,187,000	79,926,000	8,007,000	10,025,000	32,614,000
Muslims	**284,844,000**	**668,298,000**	**13,633,000**	**1,400,000**	**3,332,000**
Non-religious	2,578,000	721,113,000	57,542,000	18, 444,000	24,718,000
Hindus	1, 569,000	746,512,000	707,000	916,000	1,285,000
Buddhists	22,000	332,143,000	273,000	561,000	565,000
Atheists	**336,000**	**167,217,000**	**16,669,000**	**3,343,000**	**1,336,000**
Chinese folk Religionists	14,000	140,661,000	60,000	76,000	123,000
New Religionists	22,000	121,693,000	50,000	550,000	1,439,000
Tribe Religionists	**70,000,000**	**28, 654,000**	**1,000**	**971,000**	**41,000**
Sikhs	28,000	19,318,000	232,000	8,000	257,000
Jews	**359,000**	**6,264,000**	**1,475,000**	**1,132,000**	**6,850,000**
Shamanists	1,000	10,591,000	2,000	1,000	1,000
Confucians	1,000	6,204,000	2,000	2,000	26,000
Baha 'is	1,591,000	2,774,000	91,000	830,000	370,000
Jains	6,000	3,847,000	15,000	4,000	4,000
Shintoists	**0**	**3, 332, 000**	**1,000**	**1,000**	**1,000**
Other Religionists	461,000	12,714,000	1,475,000	3,701,000	491,000
TOTAL POPULATION	703,090,000	3,291,718,000	501,881,000	474,996,000	281,986,000

Table of all Faiths Worldwide, Mid-1993: Source: Copyright C 1994-2001 Encyclopaedia Britannica, Inc

Part One

FREEDOM TO CHOOSE IN THE CONTEXT OF THE SCRIPTURES

"I came not to call respectable people to repent, but outcasts" Luke 5:32

CHAPTER ONE

Principles of Self-knowledge

"I have come in order that you might have life - life in all its fullness." Jn 10:10

The search for happiness. What is self-renewal? Self-knowledge. Responsibilities. Conscience. Imagination. Will power. Leadership. Management. Courage. Abundance. Trust. Mysteries and Responses of the Risen Lord Jesus Christ. Know the cause within yourself and use your talent for reconstruction.

The search for Happiness

Happiness is inherent in human nature. Our Creator endows every human being with certain inalienable human rights and freedoms; among these rights and freedoms are the right to the new vision and self-renewal through faith in Jesus Christ, self-knowledge, the right to life, liberty, trust, freedom to choose, pursuit of happiness, the right to marry and found a family, free enterprise, the right to unconditional love and every necessity we need for life.

These rights and freedoms cannot be taken or abused by any public or private authority or person. The human condition is constantly improving due to self-knowledge or self-awareness. Happiness comes from being conscious of the Christ within. Jesus Christ is the same from the beginning, today and forever. Jesus Christ does not deceive and cannot be deceived by anyone.

We know only in part. We understand only in part. Then, face to face our knowledge and understanding will be full and complete. Self-knowledge is a matter of principle.

The path to happiness is self-knowledge or self-awareness. The path to self-knowledge is the wisdom of self-renewal through Christ. Seek first self-renewal and all other things will be added unto you. According to your faith, let it be unto you.

What is self-renewal?

Self-renewal is the wisdom of making holy one's physical, mental, emotional and spiritual nature in union with Christ. Self-renewal enables one to receive more energy and the grace of God to enable one to respond effectively to one's goals and responsibilities through Christ. Self-renewal is enlightenment of the whole person and freedom from the Evil One in union with Christ.

Christ himself is the physician of the body. We can trust him to heal the body. Energy flows through the physical body by the grace of God. But God helps those who help themselves.

The physical renewal of the human body can be enforced by cardio-vascular exercise. The heart and the lungs should be kept working by exercise of the body. Oxygen must continue to reach every part of the body and the brain through regular exercise of the physical body in union with Christ.

The mental nature of the human being can be renewed by exercising the mind. Regular reading and study of this book or similar book offers an aid to the renewal of our mental nature.

The emotional nature of the human being can be renewed by listening to and practising the teachings of Christ in this book or similar book. The summit of this teaching is love one another.

The spiritual nature of the human being can be renewed by daily study, reading and practising the teachings of Jesus Christ in this book or similar book. Thus, you must treat the whole text of this book as prayer for the renewal of your spiritual nature.

The whole body is the temple and abode of the Holy Spirit. The renewal of the whole body is in the control of the Holy Spirit in union with Christ.

Self-knowledge

Know thyself! If you know your self you will be able to respond effectively to your goals. Self-knowledge is a matter of principle within and without.

Self-knowledge means recognition of the endowments invested in one's soul by our Creator and ability to think and use the endowments in union with Christ. Recognition means use of the endowments. These endowments include self-knowledge, self-renewal, responsi-bilities, conscience, imagination, will power, leadership, management, courage, abundance, trust and ability to think of God and one another.

Another name for self-knowledge is self-awareness. Self-knowledge gives you the ability to freely think and choose your own value driven goals.

Self-knowledge enables you to respond to any situation. Self-knowledge gives you dominion over all things in union with Christ.

Responsibilities

The word "responsibility" is well known in management circles. The true meaning of the word is "response ability." Every day we are confronted with issues, which we must respond to. The person who can respond or has the ability to respond is an "expert."

A person who can respond will be able to earn his living. One who cannot respond cannot survive. The fittest person is the one who can respond to any situation.

But response must be proactive and not reactive. Proactive people have certain habits. They are value driven and whether it rains or shines does not make any difference to them. They can respond definitely to their goals. They participate in regular self-renewal and self-knowledge exercise. Everything they touch turns into gold. They express themselves in proactive language, e.g. "I can do it. I choose my own approach. I determine my own goals. I have an alternative solution." Proactive people can respond to any situation facing them.

On the other hand reactive people have the opposite habit. Their language betrays them. They express themselves in indefinite terms, e.g. "I can't. They made me feel horrible. I have to suffer. They will not allow me to do it. I cannot do anything about it. I am in a hopeless position." Reactive people cannot respond to the situation facing them. They follow the ugly opinion of the crowd. They are unreliable. They blame every body in the world for their failure except themselves. They imprisoned themselves in their own small world. They are not free to choose anything for themselves and others. Their goals are not value-driven. They are like Adam and Eve, who blamed the Evil One and one another.

Our Lord Jesus Christ says to these reactive people the truth shall set you free from the Evil One.

Conscience

Conscience is the ability to distinguish right from wrong. Conscience is the interior judge, jury and witness of actions. The judgement of conscience can be wrong if conscience is not properly educated or trained. Thus, we can not always rely on conscience for exercising our responsibilities. Educated, trained and well-formed conscience can help us to determine our goals, improve our weakness and actualise our goals.

Imagination

Imagination helps us to create ideas and goals first in our mind before materialisation of the goal. Thus, imagination is a key response ability inherent in the human nature. Imagination, if not trained and controlled can lead to its inability to focus on the goal.

Will power

Will power or initiative enables one to act on and achieve one's value driven goals else the goal becomes still born. Will power enables one to make a promise or commitment and keep it. Will power enables one to focus on the goal and materialise it.

Jesus Christ made a promise to us that he will send the Holy Spirit to abide with us and teach us. Christ kept that commitment and on Pentecost day the Holy Spirit descended on the Apostles. Christ never deceives and he cannot be deceived by anyone.

Leadership

Leadership is recognising the responsibility to freely choose one's goals, to determine what one wants and to reject what one does not want in union with Christ.

Management

Management is recognising the responsibility to make things happen in accord with one's value driven goals in union with Christ.

Courage

Courage is that fearless character which is prepared to take the bull by the horn. Courage confronts the solution. Courage focuses on the goal until the goal is materialised.

Abundance

There is abundance of everything within which can be materialised. There is no competition within only co-operation. There is no scarcity. There is plenty of every thing. So do not worry.

Trust

The creation is for the Creator. The creation is held by the Creator as a trustee in trust for the whole human race. The Creator himself is a beneficiary of the Creation. The whole human race is a trustee and beneficiary of the creation.

The whole human race owes a fiduciary duty to God and every individual member of the human race through Christ. The whole human race is expected to use the creation as a beneficiary of the divine trust in accord with the fiduciary obligations imposed on each member of the human race as a trustee. Nothing is mine. Everything is for the Creator.

The Creator has endowed every person with self-knowledge to enable one to respond to the talents endowed in one's soul for the benefit of God and every member of the human race through Christ. The human race is endowed with self-knowledge. Our Lord's parable of the talents is instructive.

Christ inaugurates free enterprise in union with Christ through the Lord's parable of the talents. Free enterprise means an initiative free from the Evil One.

Self-knowledge is the recognition of the response abilities of one to freely think, to determine or choose one's own value driven goals in any trade, profession, vocation, employment or family in union with Christ. The truth shall set you free from the error of the ages to enable you to determine your own goals and freely respond or choose your responsibilities through Christ.

All the foregoing endowments can be exercised through self-renewal, which leads to self-knowledge or self-awareness and enlightenment. Go on the path of self-renewal by using the small flame in you and it will expand as you go. Knowledge comes through Christ.

Mysteries and Responses of the Risen Lord Jesus Christ

Ability to respond is to be. Our role model our Lord Jesus Christ demonstrates his responses over the living and the dead.

What is a mystery? A mystery is that which is holy and is kept secret, unknown, hidden, unrevealed, unexplained to the crowd but disclosed only to few insiders, who closed their mouth and eyes and will not tell the crowd what they had heard or seen.

By persistent prayer the Father reveals all his mysteries and secrets to the faithful through Christ.

"Those who accept my commandments and obey them are the ones who love me. My Father will love those who love me; I too will love them and reveal myself to them." *Jn.14: 21.*

The risen Lord Jesus Christ is the divine person who took the form of a human being and who knows God and all his mysteries and secrets direct. He is the second Person of the Most Holy Trinity. His proactive responses speak for themselves:-

He is the Word by which God created the Universe.
He is the Word who reveals the Father to the whole human race.
He was at the side of the Father when the Universe was created.
He is the one in whom lives the fullness of divinity.
He is God from God and Light from Light.

He is the high priest who has access to the sanctuary in heaven.
He teaches with authority the Gospel truth.
He fulfils the Law by his teaching and life and resurrection.
He reveals the Christian mysteries and secrets to the faithful.
He is the fullness of revelation.

He is the goal of life.
He knows the secrets and mysteries of creation.
He knows the mysteries of the Fall and forgiveness of sin.
He knows the mysteries of salvation of the whole human race from the Evil One.
He is the Messiah sent by our Father to reveal his love for the whole human race.

He is King divine whose reign shall never end.
He walks on the water through the storm to save his Apostles.
He commands the waves and they obey him.
He brings Lazarus from death to life.
He makes the lame to walk.

He makes the dumb to speak.
He makes the deaf to hear.
He heals the sick.
He gives sight to the blind.
He drives out evil spirits.

He gives the living bread of life to those who are hungry.
He gives the living water of life to those who are thirsty.
He is the refuge of the weak and the helpless.
He blesses us all.
He instituted the seven Sacraments of his Church to enable the faithful to receive the gifts of the Holy Spirit.

He laid down his life for the salvation of the whole human race and took it back on the third day.
He is the one the faithful always encounter and adore: "My Lord and my God!"
He is the Lamb of God, which takes away the sin of the world.
He forgives every sinner who within the heart repents.
He destroyed death by his resurrection and gave us everlasting life.

He ascended to the Father and was seated at the right hand of the Father.
He and the Father sent the Holy Spirit since Pentecost day to stay with us forever to teach us the truth.
He does not deceive and cannot be deceived by any one.
He is the Amen of the Father who fulfils his promise.
He is life who gives everlasting life.

He is the way who teaches us the way to the Father.
He is the Lord who teaches us how to pray: Our Lord's prayer.
He will come again to judge the living and the dead.
He is the Law-maker, the Judge and the Jury.
Receive the Holy Spirit for your self-renewal through Christ. Amen.
Be connected to the Holy Spirit and inspiration for reconstruction. Amen.

Know the cause within yourself and use your talent for reconstruction

Know thyself! Know thy human nature! Know thy divine nature! The Kingdom of God is within you. Use the inherent talents invested in your soul by God in union with Christ for the improvement of the quality of life of the whole human race and for reconstruction.

Awake your immortal soul and spirit; your soul is of one single nature with your human body. The unity of your body and soul forms a single nature in union with the body of Christ, a temple of the Spirit.

The human being made of body and soul, is a unity, in the image and likeness of God. The body and the soul constitute the entire human person created by God. God will raise the body and the soul together of both the just and the unjust on the last day for the Last Judgement.

Your talent, mind, body with your soul is your wealth and the wealth of your country. Use your talent, mind, body and soul together in union with Christ.

How can I use my inherent talents or awaken my soul? Educate your soul in the love of God for full life on earth as in heaven. Love the Lord, your God with your mind, soul and strength and love your neighbour as Christ loves us.

That means, do not do what your human nature tells you to do but do what Jesus Christ tells you to do. Embrace the Christian values of respect for Life, Justice, Compassion, Reconciliation, Empowerment, Creativity, Humility and Service. Do that and you will help Christ to banish poverty or lack worldwide. Then, you will help Christ to install the Kingdom of God and of his love on earth as in heaven.

Your faith or lack of faith in God and in Jesus Christ is the cause of the conditions in the world. The cause is within ourselves and not in the stars. The cause is in the Creator within us and not in the created stars of the Creator. Love the Creator and your neighbour made in the image and likeness of God and not the creation. Loving the creation is idolatry.

Love is the soul of creation and creativity and a continuing creativity. That is the secret of the Christ in you.

Whoever has seen Christ has seen the Father, the Creator of heaven and earth. He is love. Through the channel of Christ one can receive all the resources of the Trinity, the Godhead. "The Father and I are one." The resources of the Father are the resources of the Son and of the Holy Spirit.

Our Lord Jesus Christ responds to our needs, "I am telling you the truth: those who believe in me will do what I do — yes, they will do even greater things, because I am going to the Father. And I will do whatever you ask for in my name, so that the Father's glory will be shown through the Son. If you ask me for anything in my name, I will do it."

Use this book daily for the way forward. This book can help you to know yourself, free yourself from doing what human nature wants you to do.

This book can help you to heal yourself, to deepen your faith in God and in Jesus Christ, renew yourself, change your vision for good.

This book can help you to practise life in the Spirit of Christ, to know where you are going, know how God thinks and makes decisions through Christ for you, for every genius and for the whole human race.

This book can help you to pray effectively *through the Scriptures*; it will help you to manage your thoughts, actions, responsibilities, emotions, talents and fulfil your goals in union with Christ; it will help you to share in the glory of God and improve the quality of your life.

According to your faith in God and in Jesus Christ, use your talents for the improvement of the quality of life of your family, and your country and the whole human race made in the likeness and image of God.

Love, faith, hope and worship of God and not the creation is the beginning of wisdom, spiritual awareness and self-knowledge. The greatest of these is love. God is love. Love transforms the world.

The Holy Spirit is the source of all inspiration and information. Be connected always to the Holy Spirit for reconsruction in your own corner.

CHAPTER TWO

Freedom to Choose

"Whoever is thirsty should come to me, and whoever believes in me should drink." Jn. 7: 37-38

Inherent Freedom to choose. Responsibility and Sin. Deliverance from Sin, death, and Law through Christ. Gifts of human Freedoms through Christ. Economic freedom to choose inspiration for reconstruction.

Inherent Freedom to Choose

Human freedom to choose one's goals is inherent in human nature as of right from the beginning of creation. Our Creator endows every human being with free will and initiative to think freely and to determine one's goals, vision and values. This human freedom to choose is confirmed through certainty of faith in the revelation of the words of the Creator:

> "You may eat the fruit of any tree in the garden,
> except the tree that gives knowledge of what is good and what is bad.
> You must not eat the fruit of that tree;
> if you do, you will die the same day." (*Gen 2: 16-17)*

Thus, we have freedom to choose to eat the fruits of any tree in the world except the fruits of the tree of duality containing the conflicts of good and evil and finally death. The tree of duality is like a mixed bag of good and evil, no and yes, likes and dislikes. One has no free choice about the fruits of the tree of duality. One has no alternative in duality of the Evil One; it is a vicious circle; one cannot win anything within that circle.

The human being is endowed with Wisdom to reject duality. Freedom means to reject duality and to love the Creator and one another and to be free to choose through Christ. Christ never deceives and cannot be deceived by anyone. The love of God and Jesus Christ is stronger than sin and death.

Responsibility and Sin

Evil came into the world because both man and woman opposed their Creator and abused the freedom to choose that the Creator endowed in man and woman. Man and woman failed to respond to their Creator.

Both man and woman were deceived by the Evil One and they ate the fruits of the "tree that gives knowledge of what is good and what is bad." This was the original sin. This first sin committed by Adam and Eve rejected the Creator and opposed the Creator.

Every man and woman must be responsible for one's conduct. Man or woman cannot blame the Evil One, or his or her partner or a third person for any ill consequences of one's conduct, action or omission.

The revelation in the Holy Bible gives us the certainty of faith in the living God that the whole of human history is marked by the original sin freely committed by our first parents, Adam and Eve. Thus sin is present in human history. Harmony with creation and God is broken.

Sin is rejection of the Creator and opposition to the Creator by any created being. Sin is an abuse of the freedom to choose that the Creator gives to created persons. That freedom to choose means that all created persons should choose to reject the Evil One and to use their endowments to love God and one another.

Deliverance from Sin, Death and Law through Christ

"Sin came into the world through one man, and his sin brought death with it. As a result, death has spread to the whole human race because everyone has sinned. There was sin in the world before the Law was given; but where there is no law, no account is kept of sins. But from the time of Adam to the time of Moses death ruled over the whole human race, even over those who did not sin in the same way that Adam did when he disobeyed God's command.

Adam was a figure of the one who was to come. But the two are not the same, because God's free gift is not like Adam's sin. It is true that many people died because of the sin of that one man. But God's grace is much greater, and so is his free gift to so many people through the grace of the one man, Jesus Christ.

And there is a difference between God's gift and the sin of one man. After the one sin, came the judgement of "Guilty"; but after so many sins, comes the undeserved gift of "Not guilty!"

It is true that through the sin of one man death began to rule because of that one man. But how much greater is the result of what was done by the one man, Jesus Christ! All who receive God's abundant grace and are freely put right with him will rule in life through Christ.

So then, as the one sin condemned all people, in the same way the one righteous act sets all people free and gives them life. And just as the mass of people were made sinners as the result of the disobedience of one man, in the same way the mass of people will all be put right with God as the result of the obedience of the one man.

Law was introduced in order to increase wrongdoing; but where sin increased, God's grace increased much more. So then, just as sin ruled by means of death, so also God's grace rules by means of righteousness, leading us to eternal life through Jesus Christ our Lord." *Rom 5: 12-21.*

The Friendship of God and Jesus Christ

God created man and woman in his image and established them in his friendship. That friendship can be lived only in free submission to the Creator. Man and woman must freely recognise the Laws of the Creator, which govern freedom to choose and respect the Laws.

Man and woman must freely trust their Creator for everything they need for survival. Man and woman are dependent on their Creator for existence. Man and woman must not allow their trust in their Creator to die in their heart. They should not abuse their freedom to choose. They should not disobey the command of their Creator.

Faith in the living God guarantees salvation and our friendship with Christ. What we must do is not to allow sin to reign. We must seek self-renewal to enable us freely to exercise our freedom to choose through Christ.

Gifts of Human Freedoms through Christ

Arising from the salvation of the whole human race by the risen Lord Jesus Christ are the gifts of human freedoms and the responsibilities through Christ. The gifts must be accepted by the faithful in order to share in the heritage and glory of God through Christ.

"I have come so that they may have full life." This life is a gift through Christ. This gift of life is sacred and should be respected by all.

The human freedoms through Christ include:-

Freedom to love God and one another. This means we must not break the Laws of God. If we commit a sin by breaking the Law, we incur the disapproval of God. We must repent, pray and ask for forgiveness. Sin makes us unclean and unholy before God.

Freedom to forgive others their sin against us so that God may forgive us our sin. This means we must restore our good relationship with God and others. The sacrament of Reconciliation is established by Christ to help us to restore good relationship or make reconciliation with God and others and to enable us to communicate with God and the whole human race.

Freedom of conscience, thought and faith in the living God. This means we must reject the Evil One and be guided by the light of faith in the living God only.

Freedom from fear of death through Christ. This means we must know that by the death and the Resurrection of Christ and his ascension to heaven, the risen Lord Jesus Christ has destroyed death and set us free from the power of the Evil One, who exercises the power of death. The faithful should no longer fear death but to treat death as the gateway to heaven for everlasting life and rest under the perpetual light.

Freedom from limitations and fear and trust in God in order to use our talents through Christ. This means we must have courage, trust in God and use the talents endowed in our soul through Christ in order to satisfy our needs through Christ. If you are in Christ, there is no limitation or fear. With faith in God everything is possible.

Freedom to accept salvation through Christ. This means we must believe in Christ and exercise prudence to follow Christ in order to know the truth. Amen.

Freedom to receive and accept the gifts of the Holy Spirit. This means we must pray for self-renewal through Christ and to participate in the sacraments established by Christ.

The gifts of the Holy Spirits are love, joy, peace, patience, kindness, goodness, faithfulness, humility and self-control. These gifts are intrinsic and, like all human rights, cannot be taken away by any person.

Economic freedom to choose for reconstruction.

The human race has the freedom to choose life in the Holy Spirit of Jesus Christ and inspiration for reconstruction and happiness. Alternatively, one could choose human culture of servitude to sin and death.

In the area of economic activity there is doubt in some countries as to how to exercise that choice. The right to choose is exercised by the people through their *freely* elected representatives in the legislative assembly. Thus, the right to vote in the election of the representatives of the people is an important human right of the people The representation of the people must be true to Christ in order to exercise a true economic freedom to choose for reconstruction. *Truth has no barrier.*

Christ is love. Love constructs. Love transforms. Love improves the quality of life of the people. But do the stewards who are chosen to represent the people in the legislative assembly, and to lead them, and to transform the people, and to account to the people know the meaning of love?

The lawmakers in the legislative assembly, and the judges who judge, and the executives who carry out the decisions of the legislature must know what is love in order to love the people as Christ loves them and not as they love them.

Embrace the Christian values of respect for human rights and justice, compassion, reconciliation, empowerment, creativity, humility and service. Do that and you will help Christ to install the Kingdom of God and of his love on earth as in heaven.

There is no opposition in the Trinity of the Godhead nor in the assembly of the people. Co-operation of all persons prevails everywhere.

The leaders of the people must lead and love them as Christ leads and loves them. The leaders of the people must know that it is their duty to reply or respond to God and the people. That is responsible government. That responsible government leads to a true economic freedom and reconstruction.

Disregard of that responsible government is idolatry. If that idolatry is legalised, in the name of the people that is also another idolatry and servitude to sin and death, which do not permit construction and improvement in the quality of life of the people.

Be connected always to the Holy Spirit of Jesus Christ, the source of all inspiration and power for improving the quality of life of the people and reconstruction.

CHAPTER THREE

The Birth of Jesus Christ for Salvation of the whole human race is stronger than human culture of sin and death

"The Kingdom of God does not come in such a way as to be seen. No one will say, "Look, here it is!" or, "There it is!; because the Kingdom of God is within you" Luke 17: 20-21

What is salvation through Jesus Christ? The Birth of Jesus is announced to the virgin Mary. The virgin Mary's Song of praise. The Birth of Jesus Christ is revealed to Joseph in a dream. The Birth of Jesus. The shepherds and the angels. The visitors from the East. The Words of Simeon. The Word of Life. John the Baptist's Message. The Lamb of God, which takes away the sin of the world. Why Everyone needs Jesus Christ for Reconstruction and happiness?

What is Salvation through Jesus Christ?

In the beginning the creation was bliss. Everything was perfect as the Creator. The Evil One came on to the stage and created a mirage and deceived the whole human race. The whole human race fell into the power of sin and death brought about by the Evil One.

Salvation comes through the love of God for the whole human race revealed through the risen Lord Jesus Christ. Salvation of the human race, like the creation, through the risen Lord Jesus Christ is a mystery.

Salvation means the risen Lord Jesus Christ, by his death and resurrection, had destroyed death and freed the souls of the whole human race from the power of the Evil One, and from sin and death. On the Cross, the risen Lord Jesus Christ took away the evil, sin, pain and suffering of the whole human race.

Our Lord brought the whole human race awake, healthy and alive to God and into the everlasting Kingdom of the living God and gave us a new faith, life, talent and Wisdom to use in order to share in the glory of God here and there.

" For it is by God's grace that you have been saved through faith. It is not the result of your own efforts, but God's gift, so that no one can boast about it." *Eph. 2: 8-9.*

Salvation of the whole human race is the only agenda of the risen Lord Jesus Christ, our Saviour. Jesus Christ, our Saviour, came down from the only true God in heaven by the power of the Holy Spirit incarnate from the womb of the virgin Mary and saved us.

By the power of the Holy Spirit, the salvation work of the risen Lord is continued for the protection of the faithful from the Evil One through the celebration of the seven Sacraments in union with Christ and in his mystical presence. Amen.

All the faithful must actively participate in the salvation works of Christ till Christ comes back. One receives salvation and renewal by faith and charity.

The faith and the response to God of the virgin Mary led to the salvation of the whole human race from the Evil One and death through Christ. Her faith in the living God has changed the whole world through Christ. The virgin Mary exercised her freedom to choose by saying yes to God. Thus, her proactive response and immediate consequences will be reproduced for self-renewal.

The Birth of Jesus is announced

"In the sixth month of Elizabeth's pregnancy God sent the angel Gabriel to a town in Galilee named Nazareth. He had a message for a young woman promised in marriage to a man named Joseph, who was a descendant of King David. Her name was Mary. The angel came to her and said, "Peace be with you! The Lord is with you and has greatly blessed you!"

Mary was deeply troubled by the angel's message, and she wondered what his words meant. The angel said to her, Don't be afraid, Mary; God has been gracious to you. You will become pregnant and give birth to a son, and you will name him Jesus. He will be great and will be called the Son of the Most High God. The Lord God will make him a king, as his ancestor David was, and he will be the king of the descendant of Jacob for ever; his kingdom will never end!"

Mary said to the angel, "I am a virgin. How, then, can this be?" The angel answered, "The Holy Spirit will come on you, and God's power will rest upon you. For this reason the holy child will be called the Son of God. Remember your relative Elizabeth. It is said that she cannot have children, but she herself is now six months pregnant, even though she is very old. For there is nothing that God cannot do." *Lk 1: 26- 37.*

"I am the Lord's servant," said Mary;
"may it happen to me as you have said."

And the angel left her. *Lk 1: 38.*

The Virgin Mary's Song of Praise

"My heart praises the Lord;
My soul is glad because of God my Saviour,
For he has remembered me, his lowly servant!
From now on all people will call me happy,
because of the great things
The mighty God has done for me.

His name is holy;
from one generation to another
he shows mercy to those who honour him.

He has stretched out his mighty arm
and scattered the proud with all their plans.

He has brought down mighty kings
from their thrones, and lifted up the lowly.

He has filled the hungry with good things,
and sent the rich away with empty hands.

He has kept the promise he made to our ancestors,
and has come to the help of his servant Israel.

He has remembered to show mercy to Abraham
and to all his descendants for ever." Lk 1: 46-55.

The Birth of Jesus Christ is revealed to Joseph in a Dream

"This was how the birth of Jesus Christ took place. His mother Mary was engaged to Joseph, but before they were married, she found out that she was going to have a baby by the Holy Spirit.

Joseph was a man who always did what was right, but he did not want to disgrace Mary publicly; so he made plans to break the engagement privately. While he was thinking of this, an angel of the Lord appeared to him in a dream and said, "Joseph, descendant of David, do not be afraid to take Mary to be your wife. For it is by the

Holy Spirit that she conceived. She will have a son, and you will name him Jesus – because he will save his people from their sins."

Now all this happened in order to make what the Lord had said through the prophet come true. "A virgin will become pregnant and have a son, and he will be called Immanuel" (which means, "God with us").

So when Joseph woke up, he married Mary, as the angel of the Lord had told him to do. But he had no sexual relations with her before she gave birth to her son. And Joseph named him Jesus." *Mat 1: 18-25.*

The Birth of Jesus

"At that time the Emperor Augustus ordered a census to be taken throughout the Roman Empire. When this first census took place, Quirinius was the governor of Syria. Everyone, then, went to register himself, each to his own town.

Joseph went from the town of Nazareth in Galilee to the town of Bethlehem in Judea, the birth-place of King David. Joseph went there because he was a descendant of David. He went to register with Mary, who was promised in marriage to him. She was pregnant, and while they were in Bethlehem, the time came for her to have her baby. She gave birth to her first son, wrapped him in strips of cloth and laid him in a manger – there was no room for them to stay in the inn." *Lk 2: 1-7.*

The Shepherds and the Angels

"There were some shepherds in that part of the country who were spending the night in the fields, taking care of their flocks. An angel of the Lord appeared to them, and the glory of the Lord shone over them. They were terribly afraid, but the angel said to them:

"Don't be afraid! I am here with good news for you, which will bring great joy to all the people. This very day in David's town your Saviour was born – Christ the Lord! And this is what will prove it to you: you will find a baby wrapped in strips of cloth and lying in a manger."

Suddenly a great army of heaven's angels appeared with the angels, singing praises to God:

> "Glory to God in the highest heaven,
> and peace on earth to those with
> whom he is pleased!"

When the angels went away from them back into heaven, the shepherds said to one another, "Let's go to Bethlehem and see this thing that has happened, which the Lord has told us."

So they hurried off and found Mary and Joseph and saw the baby lying in the manger. When the shepherds saw him, they told them what the angel had said about the child. All who heard it were amazed at what the shepherds said. Mary remembered all these things and thought deeply about them.

The shepherds went back, singing praises to God for all they had heard and seen; it had been just as the angel had told them." *Lk 2: 8-20.*

The visitors from the East.

Jesus was born to save the whole human race from their sin. The three wise men who studied the stars came from the East to Bethlehem. When they saw the child with his mother Mary, they knelt down and worshipped him. They presented gifts of gold, frankincense and myrrh to the child.

The Words of Simeon

On the day of presentation for purification and dedication of Christ to the Lord in the Temple at Jerusalem, Simeon took the baby Jesus in his arms, gave thanks to God and said:

> " Now, Lord, you have kept your promise,
> and you may let your servant go in peace.
> With my own eyes I have seen your salvation,
> which you have prepared in the presence of all peoples:
> A light to reveal your will to the Gentiles
> and bring glory to your people Israel." Lk 2: 29-32

Simeon blessed Mary and Joseph and said to Mary: "This child is chosen by God for the destruction and the salvation of many in Israel. He will be a sign from God, which many people will speak against and so reveal their secret thoughts. And sorrow, like a sharp sword, will break your own heart." *Lk 2: 34-35*

The Word of Life

In the beginning the Word already existed; the Word was with God, and the Word was God. From the very beginning the Word was with God. Through him God made all things; not one thing in all creation was made without him. The Word was made the source of life, and this life brought light to humanity. The light shines in the darkness, and the darkness has never put it out.

God sent his messenger, a man named John, who came to tell people about the light, so that all should hear the message and believe. He himself was not the light; he came to tell about the light. This was the real light – the light that comes into the world and shines on everyone.

The Word was in the world, and though God made the world through him, yet the world did not recognise him. He came to his own country, but his own people did not receive him. Some, however, did receive him and believed in him; so he gave them the right to become God's children. They did not become God's children by natural means, that is, by being born as the children of a human father; God himself was their Father.

The Word became a human being and, full of grace and truth, lived among us. We saw his glory, the glory, which he received as the Father's only Son.

John spoke about him. He cried out, "This is the one I was talking about when I said, "He comes after me, but he is greater than I am, because he existed before I was born."

Out of the fullness of his grace he has blessed us all, giving us one blessing after another. God gave the Law through Moses, but grace and truth came through Jesus Christ. No one has ever seen God. The only Son, who is the same as God and is at the Father's side, he has made him known.

John the Baptist's Message

"The Jewish authorities in Jerusalem sent some priests and Levites to John, to ask him, "Who are you?"

John did not refuse to answer, but spoke out openly and clearly, saying: "I am not the Messiah"

"Who are you, then?" they asked. "Are you Elijah?" "No, I am not," John answered. "Are you the Prophet?" they asked. "No," he replied. "Then tell us who you are," they said. "We have to take an answer back to those who sent us. What do you say about yourself?" John answered by quoting the prophet Isaiah:

" I am the voice of someone shouting in the desert: Make a straight path for the Lord to travel!"

The messengers, who had been sent by the Pharisees, then asked John, "If you are not the Messiah nor Elijah nor the Prophet, why do you baptize?"

John answered, "I baptize with water, but among you stands the one you do not know. He is coming after me, but I am not good enough even to untie his sandals."

All this happened in Bethany on the east side of the River Jordan, where John was baptizing."

The Lamb of God, which takes away the sin of the world.

"The next day John saw Jesus coming to him, and said, "There is the Lamb of God, who takes away the sin of the world! This is the one I was talking about when I said, " A man is coming after me, but he is greater than I am, because he existed before I was born." I did not know who he would be, but I came baptizing with water in order to make him known to the people of Israel.

And John gave this testimony: "I saw the Spirit come down like a dove from heaven and stay on him. I still did not know that he was the one, but God, who sent me to baptize with water, had said to me, "You will see the Spirit come down and stay on a man; he is the one who baptizes with the Holy Spirit." I have seen it, said John, and I tell you that he is the Son of God." *Jn 1: 1-34*

Why Everyone needs Jesus Christ for Reconstruction and Happiness

Jesus Christ is a necessity for life and inspiration for reconstruction on earth as in heaven because he is love. The love of God for the whole human race and one another as God loves us, is revealed to us through only Christ.

Through Christ, everything is possible. Jesus Christ, the only begotten Son of his Father, was sent by his Father in heaven to set us free, save and liberate us from the Evil One and deliver us to God after the original sin and the Fall of Adam and Eve. He came to do his Father's will and not his own will. He suffered with us and experienced human nature and human suffering after the Fall so that we can also experience and know God and share in the divine nature of Christ and the glory of God.

Christ sets us free and died on the cross instead of us to carry away our culture of sin and death against God.

Christ sets us free and obtained the forgiveness of God for our sins against God. He came to forgive sin. He came to set death aside. He came to set aside error.

Christ sets us free and restores a good relationship and intimacy between the whole human race and God. Christ sets us free from guilt before God. Every human being is guilty before God because we break, by our thought, word, deed and omission, the Laws of God inscribed in our heart. No one can plead ignorance of the Law of God.

Christ, who shares our human nature, sets us free from fear of death, and set aside death, and defeated the Evil One, who held the power of death over the whole human race. The Evil One can no longer deceive any one of the nature of death. The Evil One misleads us that death is an end and we should not bother about God. Christ by his Resurrection teaches us that death is the gateway of the faithful to heaven for everlasting life. Christ can help those who suffer and are tempted by the Evil One, because he himself was tempted and put to the test by the Evil One and he passed through suffering. (Hebrews 2: 14-18).

Christ sets us free to love God and one another because God first loves us and sent his only begotten Son to be the means by which our sins are forgiven. Whoever, does not love, does not know God. God is love. (1 John 4: 7-19).

Christ sets us free to know and worship God. God is Spirit. People can worship God only by the power of his Holy Spirit as he truly is. (John 4: 24)

Christ sets us free but did not leave us orphans but he sent his Holy Spirit to abide with us, to teach us and guide us as to the truth about God.

Christ sets us free in order that we should change ourselves through the Holy Spirit of Christ. The Holy Spirit of Christ in us produces love, joy, peace, patience, kindness, goodness, faithfulness, humility, self-control and self-renewal. The Holy Spirit, the Lord, the giver of life, has given us life and health; he must also control our life and health. (Galatians 5: 22-25).

Christ sets us free and filled our emptiness and the void in us with life in the Holy Spirit of Christ.

Christ sets us free and restored our faith in God and in himself so that we should not perish with the Evil One but enter everlasting life.

Christ sets us free so that we can accept his free gift of love to us and invite the Holy Spirit of Christ to live in us. It is a free gift; we have not given any consideration to God for it; we do not earn it, deserve it, merit it, nor are we worthy of it. Sinful as we are, we cannot match the love of God for us. God loves the whole human race because he is true and faithful to his own nature through only Christ.

Christ sets us free so that we can think correctly in union with Christ. Christ sets us free so that we can make decisions in union with Christ.

Christ sets us free to teach us repentance; to teach us how to ask for forgiveness for our sins, and how to make decisions not to sin again and to avoid the culture of sin and death against God and one another.

Christ sets us free so that we can remain in him free from sin and holy forever. Christ sets us free so that we, as branches of the vine in unity with him, the vine, and his Father as the gardener, can inherit the Kingdom of God.

Christ Resurrected to the Father and was seated at the right hand of the Father. From where he will come to judge the living and the dead.

Christ achieved forgiveness for human sins by his Father. Christ is the second person of the Most Holy Trinity, God from God and Light from Light.

No one can enter the Kingdom of God except by permission and grace of Christ. The faithful always experience and encounter the presence of Christ.

God is Spirit. God is love. Love of God comes to the whole human race only through Christ

CHAPTER FOUR

The Resurrection of Jesus Christ and Life after Death

"I am the resurrection and the life. Those who believe in me will live, even though they die; and all those who live and believe in me will never die" Jn 11: 25-26

The Resurrection of Jesus Christ and the Empty Tomb. Jesus appeared first to the women who went to the Tomb: Mary Magdalene, and Joanna, and Salome, and Mary, the Mother of James. The Report of the Soldiers Guarding the Tomb and the Bribe Money of the Chief Priests. Jesus appeared to his Eleven Disciples and the Apostolic Commission. Unity of the Apostolic Commission and the Farewell Summit Declaration of Jesus Christ: " I am the Way; I am Truth and Life. No one can come to the Father except through me." The Vision of the Last Judgement of Jesus Christ. The Particular Judgement and Life after Death. The Last Judgement and Life after Death.

The Resurrection of Jesus Christ and the Empty Tomb

The first stories were of an empty tomb. Jesus was seen by Mary Magdalene, Peter, the twelve Apostles and more than 500 of his followers at once. *1 Cor 15: 5-6.*

After the resurrection Christ can touch people and eat meals with them. He is not a ghost. The risen body of Christ is the same body, which was tortured and crucified, and it still bears the traces of the Passion.

This authentic real body possesses the new properties of a glorious body: which is not limited by space and time but able to be present where and when he wills. Christ's humanity is no longer confined to earth, and it belongs after the resurrection only to the Father's divine realm in heaven.

The risen body of Christ passes from the state of death to another life beyond time and space. No one can say how it happened physically. No one saw it happen.

The Resurrection of Christ means, by his death, Christ liberates the whole human race from sin; he opens for the whole human race the way to a new life. Christ's Resurrection is the principle source of the future resurrection of the whole human race. The glorified body of Christ ascends to heaven and is seated at the right hand of his Father. The Resurrection event is for self-renewal and reconstruction. "After the Sabbath, as Sunday morning was dawning, Mary Magdalene and the other Mary went to look at the tomb. Suddenly there was a violent earthquake; an angel of the Lord came down from heaven, rolled the stone away, and sat on it. His appearance was like lightening, and his clothes were white as snow. The guards were so afraid that they trembled and became like dead men.

The angel spoke to the women. "You must not be afraid," he said. "I know you are looking for Jesus, who was crucified. He is not here; he has been raised, just as he said. Come here and see the place where he was lying. Go quickly now, and tell his disciples, "He has been raised from death, and now he is going to Galilee ahead of you; there you will see him!" Remember what I have told you."

So they left the tomb in a hurry, afraid and yet filled with joy, and ran to tell his disciples.

Jesus appeared first to the Women who went to the Tomb: Mary Magdalene, and Joanna, and Salome, and Mary, the Mother of James

Suddenly Jesus met them and said, "Peace be with you." They came up to him, took hold of his feet, and worshipped him. "Do not be afraid, Jesus said to them. "Go and tell my brothers to go to Galilee, and there they will see me."

The Report of the Soldiers Guarding the Tomb and the Bribe Money of the Chief Priests.

"While the women went on their way, some of the soldiers guarding the tomb went back to the city and told the chief priests everything that had happened. The chief priests met with the elders and made their plan; they gave a large sum of money to the soldiers and said, "You are to say that his disciples came during the night and stole his body while you were asleep. And if the Governor should hear of this, we will convince him that you are innocent, and you will have nothing to worry about."

The guards took the money and did what they were told to do. And so that is the report spread round by the Jews to this very day."

Jesus appeared to his Eleven Disciples and the Apostolic Commission

"The eleven disciples went to the hill in Galilee where Jesus had told them to go. When they saw him, they worshipped him, even though some of them doubted.

Jesus drew near and said to them, "I have been given all authority in heaven and on earth. Go, then, to all peoples everywhere and make them my disciples: baptise them in the name of the Father, the Son, and the Holy Spirit, and teach them to obey everything I have commanded you. And I will be with you always, to the end of the age."(Matt 28: 1-20)

"Go throughout the whole world and preach the gospel to the whole human race. Whoever believes and is baptised will be saved; whoever does not believe will be condemned. Believers will be given the power to perform miracles: they will drive out demons in my name; they will speak in strange tongues; if they pick up snakes or drink any poison, they will not be harmed; they will place their hands on sick people, who will get well." (Mark 16: 15-18)

Unity of the Apostolic Commission and the Farewell Summit Declaration of Jesus Christ: "I am the Way; I am Truth and Life. No one can come to the Father except through me"

Christ asserts his authority in heaven and on earth after his Resurrection. This is evident when he said: "I have been given all authority in heaven and on earth."

This declaration of authority is the same as the authority he asserted in his Farewell Summit Declaration when he said: "I am the Way; I am Truth and Life. No one can come to the Father except through me."

Thus, Christ repeated his message of love and salvation to the whole human race in order to emphasise the importance of the message.

The two declarations are addressed to the whole human race through the Apostles. Seven points emerge from the Apostolic Commission Declaration:-

1. "I have been given all authority in heaven and on earth. The emphasis is on *all authority* without limitation and it encompasses the authority in the Farewell Summit Declaration. That authority is love.

2. "Go, then, to all peoples of everywhere and make them my disciples. The same command is expressed when he said: "Go throughout the world and preach the gospel to the whole human race." Preaching the gospel means spreading the Good News of the love of God for the whole human race and salvation from the culture of sin and death through Christ..

3. "Baptise them in the name of the Father, the Son, and the Holy Spirit." This mandate is a call to carry out the first sacrament of initiation of the believers into the Church of Christ. Baptism takes away all the sins of the recipient up to the date of Baptism.

4. "And teach them to obey everything I have commanded you." The Church has been faithfully carrying out the teaching. But the people are not easy to teach. Not everything Christ has commanded is being obeyed. The offenders include, 1. The Multinational Corporations, which misuse the technological revolution against Christ. Worldly interests and life in the Holy Spirit of Christ are not mutually exclusive. Both must be harmonised and integrated for the glory of only God and not the creation. 2. The Bankers, whose lending policies are anti-Christ and loaded against the poor and the love of God and our neighbour, as Christ loves us. 3. The Sovereign State, whose policies and statute are against the Ten Commandments. They abuse human rights and the love of God and our neighbour, as Christ loves us. 4. The Media, whose manifestations are against the spirit of the Ten Commandments, 5. Dividers of the

Church, the body of Christ. The body of Christ must remain united for the love of Christ and not divided. Who made you a divider of the inheritance? God is indivisible. The love of God is indivisible! Lord, be quick with ecumenism. 6. Individuals must stop it, and to listen to Christ and obey his commandments of love. 7. The matrimonial partners must fulfil their family obligations in love in union with Christ. These seven groups disobey the authority of Christ every day. All disobedience is idolatry.

5. "Whoever believes and is baptised will be saved; whoever does not believe will be condemned." Christ is again reminding us of his Judgement for everlasting life in heaven or hell.

6. "Believers will be given the power to perform miracles: they will drive out demons in my name; they will speak in strange tongues; if they pick up snakes or drink any poison, they will not be harmed; they will place their hands on sick people, who will get well." These are gifts of Christ to believers. We need prayer in life in the Holy Spirit of Christ to exercise these gifts.

7. "And I will be with you always, to the end of the age." The end of the age is the end of our world. Christ will then hand over the Kingdom to his Father. We are in the presence of Christ all the time and he is with us always. He is faithful. Are we faithful to Christ?

The Farewell Summit Declaration of Christ is examined in chapter five of this book.

The Vision of the Last Judgement of Jesus Christ

"When the Son of Man comes as King and all the angels with him, he will sit on his royal throne, and the people of all nations will be gathered before him. Then he will divide them into two groups, just as the shepherd separates the sheep from the goats.

He will put the righteous people on his right and the others on his left. Then the King will say to the people on his right "Come, you that are blessed by my Father! Come and possess the kingdom, which has been prepared for you ever since the creation of the world. I was hungry and you fed me, thirsty and you gave me a drink; I was a stranger and you received me in your homes, naked and you clothed me; I was sick and you took care of me, in prison and you visited me."

The righteous will then answer him, "When, Lord, did we ever see you hungry and feed you, or thirst and give you a drink? When did we ever see you a stranger and welcome you in our homes, or naked and clothe you? When did we ever see you sick or in prison, and visit you? The King will reply, "I tell you, whenever you did this for one of the least important of these members of my family, you did it for me!"

Then he will say to those on his left, "Away from me, you that are under God's curse! Away to the eternal fire which has been prepared for the Devil and his angels! I was hungry but you would not feed me, thirsty but you would not give me a drink. I was a stranger but you would not welcome me in your homes, naked but you would not clothe me; I was sick and in prison but you would not take care of me."

Then they will answer him, "When, Lord, did we ever see you hungry or thirsty or a stranger of naked or sick or in prison, and would not help you?" The King will reply, "I tell you, whenever you refused to help one of these least important ones, you refused to help me." These, then, will be sent off to eternal punishment, but the righteous will go to eternal life. *Mat 25: 31-46.*

The Particular Judgement and Life after Death

Every person receives his eternal reward in his or her immortal soul at the very moment of his or her death, in a particular Judgement. The particular Judgement refers one's life to Christ.

In particular Judgement, one will either go to heaven through purification in purgatory or direct to heaven immediately or to hell immediately. But we do not know any one who has gone to hell so far. The prospect is threatening enough and every one must repent now and follow Christ.

Those who die in the grace and friendship of God and are perfectly purified, live forever with Christ in heaven. They are like God forever. They see God as he is face to face.

The Last Judgement and Life after Death

The resurrection of all the dead, of both the just and the unjust, will precede the Last Judgement.

The reign of Christ is yet to be fulfilled with power and glory by the King's return to earth to judge the living and the dead. Christ will come in his glory. The whole human race will be united. Nobody knows the hour except God.

The present time is a time of the Holy Spirit and of witness. The time is marked with the trial of the Evil One.

This time is the time of waiting and watching. The conduct, action and omission of every one and the secrets of hearts will be brought to light.

Christ is the Law-maker, the Judge and the grand Jury. By choosing to reject the grace of God in this life, one already judges oneself.

Part Two

THE PROFESSION OF THE CHRISTIAN FAITH FOR SELF-RENEWAL

"For God loved the world so much that he gave his only Son, so that everyone who believes in him may not die but have eternal life" Jn 3:16

CHAPTER FIVE

The Profession of the Christian Faith in the living God through the Most Holy Trinity

"If you had faith as big as a mustard seed, you could say to this mulberry tree, "Pull yourself up by the roots and plant yourself in the sea!" and it would obey you" Luke 16:6

What is faith in the invisible living God? Nature of God and of the Most Holy Trinity. The Apostles' Creed. The Nicene Creed. Faith in God is accepting the invitation of God to his Son's wedding Feast. The Farewell Summit Declaration of Jesus Christ: I am the Way; I am Truth and Life. No one can come to the Father except through me." God's Glory in Creation. The Law of the Lord is Perfect.

What is Faith in the invisible Living God?

In the name of the Father, and of the Son, and of the Holy Spirit. Amen. The invisible living God reveals himself in the fullness of his love and glory to the whole human race through only our risen Lord Jesus Christ. Our Lord saved us and invited us into his Kingdom to share with him his Father's heritage and glory. The response of the whole human race to our Lord's invitation is faith in the invisible, living God through the risen Lord Jesus Christ.

Faith in God means we must surrender our soul, thought, action and will to the will of the living God only through the risen Lord Jesus Christ. It is through faith in the invisible, living God by the Virgin Mary that the Virgin Mary conceived by the power of the Holy Spirit and the whole human race was saved by Christ from sin, death and the Evil One.

What is faith? "To have faith is to be sure of the things we hope for, to be certain of the things we cannot see. It was by their faith that people of ancient times won God's approval. It is by faith that we understand that the universe was created by God's word, so that what can be seen was made out of what cannot be seen." *Heb 11: 1-3.*

Our risen Lord Jesus Christ is the final, full and true revelation of the invisible, living God. "In the past, God spoke to our ancestors many times and in many ways through the prophets, but in these last days he has spoken to us through his Son. He is the one through whom God created the universe, the one whom God has chosen to posses all things at the end. He reflects the brightness of God's glory and is the exact likeness of God's own being, sustaining the universe with his powerful word. After achieving forgiveness for human sins, he sat down in heaven at the right-hand side of God, the Supreme Power." *Heb 1: 1-3.*

Faith is acceptance of certain supernatural truths by the faithful because of their supernatural authority. In Christianity, faith is the acceptance of the relationship between the Most Holy Trinity and the believer or follower of Christ. In that relationship the Trinity discloses and communicates itself and the believer proactively responds to the self-communication and self-revelation of the Trinity by making total commitment to the revelation and the communication. The practical result is love of God and one another, as Christ loves us; a changed life style of the faithful.

Faith in God means ability to exercise with prudence the huge capital of talent, wisdom, responsibilities and reward endowed in our soul through Christ.

Nature of God and of the Most Holy Trinity

In the name of the Father, and of the Son, and of the Holy Spirit. Amen. O! Blessed Most Holy Trinity, thy Kingdom come by the grace of our risen Lord. Grant us the grace to understand communication and revelation of yourself to us. Your divine Trinity is one and indivisible God.

We believe the divine Trinity is one God in three persons: Father, and the Son, and the Holy Spirit. The three divine persons: Father, and the Son, and the Holy Spirit do not share one God between themselves but *each of the three divine persons is God whole, entire and perfect.* Thus, Christ is true God from true God, Light from Light.

The Father is that which the Son is, and the Son is that which the Father is, and the Father and the Son are that which the Holy Spirit is. The Trinity is one and indivisible and by substance one living God.

Our Lord revealed the secret of the Father to us when he said:

"Whoever has seen me has seen the Father." *Jn 14: 9.*

The three divine persons are different from one another in relation to their indivisible origin and in performance of their common functions according to one's unique personal responsibility. God is one but not a loner in action. God has a company through which he carries out his personal responsibilities.

The Father is the creator of heaven and earth and the generator of the whole human race in the presence of the Son and the Holy Spirit.

The Son is he who was at the side of the Father at the time of the creation and He is the only begotten Son incarnate of the Father, who was sent by the Father to die for us on the Cross, to take away our sins, and to save us from the Evil One and his empty promises through the resurrection and victory over the Evil One by our risen Lord.

The Holy Spirit, is he who was with the Father and the Son from the beginning of the creation, and who proceeds from the Father and the Son to shower on us his abundant grace and truth to enable us remain justified and holy in the name of our risen Lord.

The three divine persons are linked in unity and related to one another in the divine Trinity and there is no opposition or division but only perfect peace and harmony in the divine Trinity.

By reason of that unity of the Trinity, the Father is wholly and entirely in the Son and in the Holy Spirit. The Son is wholly and entirely in the Father and in the Holy Spirit. The Holy Spirit is wholly and entirely in the Father and wholly and entirely in the Son. The unity and glory of the three divine persons in the Blessed Most Holy Trinity is everlasting.

"Do you not believe, Philip, that I am in the Father and the Father is in me? The words that I have spoken to you, Jesus said to his disciples, do not come from me. The Father, who remains in me, does his own work. Believe me when I say that I am in the Father and the Father is in me. If not, believe because of the things I do." *Jn 14: 10-11.* "The Father and I are one" *Jn 10: 30.*

The divine Trinity reveals itself and the beginning and the end of the creation. No created being can reveal the secret of the divine Trinity and the beginning and the end of the creation. Amen.

The Apostles' Creed

I believe in God the Father almighty, creator of heaven and earth.
I believe in Jesus Christ, his only Son, our Lord.

He was conceived by the power of the Holy Spirit and born of the Virgin Mary.
He suffered under Pontius Pilate, was crucified, died, and was buried.
He descended to the dead. On the third day he rose again.
He ascended into heaven and is seated at the right hand of the Father.
He will come again to judge the living and the dead.
I believe in the Holy Spirit,
the holy catholic Church, the communion of saints,
the forgiveness of sins,
the resurrection of the body,
and the life everlasting. Amen.

The Nicene Creed

We believe in one God, the Father, the Almighty, maker of heaven and earth, of all that is, seen and unseen.
We believe in one Lord, Jesus Christ, the only Son of God, eternally begotten of the Father, God from God, Light from Light, true God from true God, begotten, not made, of one Being with the Father. Through him all things were made.
For us men and for our salvation, he came down from heaven: by the power of the Holy Spirit, he became incarnate of the Virgin Mary, and became man.
For our sake he was crucified under Pontius Pilate; he suffered death and was buried.
On the third day he rose again in accordance with the Scriptures;
he ascended into heaven and is seated at the right hand of the Father.
He will come again in glory to judge the living and the dead, and his kingdom will have no end.
We believe in the Holy Spirit, the Lord, the giver of life, who proceeds from the Father and the Son. With the Father and the Son he is worshipped and glorified. He has spoken through the Prophets.
We believe in one holy catholic and apostolic Church.
We acknowledge one baptism for the forgiveness of sins.
We look for the resurrection of the dead,
and the life of the world to come. Amen.

Faith in God is Accepting the Invitation of God to his Son's Wedding Feast

"Jesus again used parables in talking to the people. The Kingdom of heaven is like this. Once there was a king who prepared a wedding feast for his son. He sent his servants to tell the invited guests to come to the feast, but they did not want to come. So he sent other servants with this message for the guests: "My feast is ready now; my bullocks and prize calves have been butchered, and everything is ready. Come to the wedding feast!"

But the invited guests paid no attention and went about their business: one went to his farm, another to his shop, while others grabbed the servants, beat them, and killed them. The king was very angry; so he sent his soldiers, who killed those murderers and burnt down their city.

Then he called his servants and said to them, "My wedding feast is ready, but the people I invited did not deserve it. Now go to the main streets and invite to the feast as many people as you find." So the servants went out into the streets and gathered all the people they could find, good and bad alike; and the wedding hall was filled with people.

The king went in to look at the guests and saw a man who was not wearing wedding clothes. "*Friend, how did you get in here without wedding clothes?*" (*Italics mine*) the king asked him. But the man said nothing. Then the king told the servants, "Tie him up hand and foot, and throw him outside in the dark. There he will cry and grind his teeth."

And Jesus concluded, "Many are invited, but few are chosen." *Mat 22: 1-14.*

The Farewell Summit Declaration of Jesus Christ: "I am the Way; I am Truth and Life. No one can come to the Father except through me"

1. What is the Scriptural source of this Farewell Summit Declaration?

"I am the Way; I am Truth and Life.
No one can come to the Father
except through me." John 14: 6 (JB).

This emphatic declaration is the central statement of faith in the

Most Holy Trinity and salvation of the whole human race through only Christ. In this farewell declaration, Jesus Christ, our Saviour, discussed the last four things: death, judgement, everlasting life or love in heaven or hell. There is no salvation or everlasting life or love outside Jesus Christ, because Christ is love.

The declaration means no being, seen or unseen, can get access to the Father in the Kingdom of heaven for everlasting life unless by the permission, decision, judgement or the grace of Christ. Every one will be referred to the King on one's death for the Particular and Last Judgement. See chapter four on the Particular and Last Judgement.

Christ is the Way to the Father. He is Truth and Life. The Way became merged with the Truth and the Life. The Truth is love. The Life is love. The Way is love. Love is God.

Every prayer can be answered only through Christ.

2. Who made this declaration?

This declaration was made by our Saviour Jesus Christ, the Founder of the Christian Church, the Body of Christ.

"Jesus is the one of whom the scripture says: "The stone that you the builders despised turned out to be the most important of all." Salvation is to be found through him alone; in all the world there is no one else whom God has given who can save us." Acts 4: 11-12.

"How, then, shall we escape if we pay no attention to such a great salvation? The Lord himself first announced this salvation, and those who heard him proved to us that it is true. At the same time God added his witness to theirs by performing all kinds of miracles and wonders and by distributing the gifts of the Holy Spirit according to his will." (Heb. 2: 3-4)

"For there is one God, and there is one who brings God and human beings together, the man Christ Jesus, who gave himself to redeem everyone." (1 Tim 2: 5-6)

He is the only one God raised from the dead. See chapter four on his Resurrection. See chapter one on the general responses of Christ Jesus, our Saviour.

3. In what capacity did Jesus make this declaration?

Firstly, in his capacity as the messenger of the living God. Secondly, as the second person of the Most Holy Trinity. Thirdly, as the King in the Kingdom of God. Fourthly, as the Judge in the Particular and Last Judgement after death.

4. When did Jesus make this declaration?

This declaration was made at the final stage of his salvation mission in a farewell dialogue between him and his disciples in preparation for his arrest, crucifixion, death and resurrection to the Father.

The dialogue came after the Last Supper. At the table of the Last Supper he washed the feet of his disciples and requested them to do the same and wash the feet of each other. At that Last Supper, Jesus dipped a piece of bread in the dish and gave it to Judas Iscariot and after Judas had taken the bread, Satan entered him and he left the table to betray Jesus.

The declaration is the direct answer to a question put to Jesus by Thomas in the farewell dialogue when he said: "Lord, we do not know where you are going, so how can we know the way?

After that declaration in response to Thomas, Jesus discussed the nature of the Trinity, the Godhead, with the disciples without referring to the word "Trinity." He went on to reveal his Father, "Anyone who has seen me has seen the Father." He went on to reveal his divinity as the second person of the Trinity when he said, "I am in the Father and the Father is in me" He went on and revealed the third person of the Trinity, "I shall ask the Father, and he will give you another Paraclete to be with you for ever, the Spirit of truth whom the world can never accept since it neither sees nor knows him; but you know him, because he is with you. I shall not leave you orphans. I shall come to you" (John 14: 9, 11, 16-18) JB.

Christ has died. Christ is risen. Christ will come again. The second person of the Trinity will come again and he will not leave you orphans.

Christ further called on the whole human race to live their lives in the Spirit of Christ. You must be born again. That means life rooted in the Spirit of Christ and shared with Christ. Christ is the real vine and the whole human race are the branches and his Father and our Father is the gardener. Christ said, our Father, the gardener, breaks off every branch in him that does not bear fruit, and he prunes every branch that does bear fruit, so that it will be clean and holy and bear much fruit. Those who remain united with Christ, and Christ is in them, will bear much fruit. We cannot do anything unless we are with Christ. We cannot go to the Father except though Christ.

5. To whom was the declaration addressed?

The declaration was addressed initially to the disciples and secondly to the whole human race.

6. What is the importance of the declaration for the whole human race?

Christ, the King, declared the rule of law in his Kingdom in heaven, where he is the only Judge, Jury and Prosecutor. Christ is the only way to the Father. There is no salvation outside Christ.

7. Has the declaration a binding force of Law in the Kingdom of God?

Yes, it is strictly enforceable on the death of everyone in the Particular and the Last Judgement by Christ.

8. What is the meaning of "I am"?

By "I am" Christ is referring to the "Most Holy Trinity" and in particular his Father, the first person of the Trinity. Christ does not do anything by his own authority only by the authority of his Father and with his Holy Spirit. There is no opposition in the Trinity; harmony prevails.

Christ Jesus said, "When you lift up the Son of Man, you will know that "I Am Who I Am; then you will know that I do nothing on my own authority, but I say only what the Father has instructed me to say." Thus, the declaration was made by Christ as he was instructed by the Father to say.

"I am what I am" is "He who is" or another name for the Creator, the Cause of being. Yahweh is the personal name of the Creator revealed to Moses. Yahweh, the name of God, is holy and too sacred to be pronounced. Thus, only the consonants YHWH were written by the Jews to revere God.

9. What does he mean by I am "the Way"?

By the use of "the Way" Christ is referring to all his teachings of salvation, Commandments, his sacramental mandates to the disciples and the faithful and above all his Command to love one another. He is the only Way to the Father. He opened the gateway to the Father by his life, death and Resurrection. If not Christ, who did it? He is now seated at the right hand of the Father in heaven with the wounds of the Passion. From there he will come again to judge the living and the dead.

10. What does he mean by I am "Truth"

He is the final and full Truth of his Father. Any other truth before and after Christ is intermediate and partial. Where the full Truth appears all other truths cease to exist.

The truth will set you free. Jesus said, "If you obey my teaching, you are really my disciples; you will know the truth, and the truth will set you free" from slavery to sin.

God is Spirit. God is everywhere. God knows and hears everything. God is Truth. It is only when we obey the teachings of Christ, pray to God and worship God in Spirit that we shall know God.

Jesus said, I am telling you the truth: those who hear my words and believe in him who sent me have eternal life. They will not be judged, but have already passed from death to life. I am telling you the truth: the time is coming — the time has already come — when the dead will hear the voice of the Son of God, and those who hear it will come to life. Just as the Father is himself the source of life, in the same way he has made his Son to be the source of life. And he has given the Son the right to judge, because he is the Son of Man. Do not be surprised at this; the time is coming when all the dead will hear his voice and come out of their graves: those who have done good will rise and live, and those who have done evil will rise and be condemned. (Jn 5: 24-29)

The declaration is the salvation statement of Christ. It is salvation statement of our freedom from the Evil One, freedom from slavery to sin, in the Holy Spirit of Christ.

11. What does he mean by I am "Life"?

He means everlasting life, life in the Holy Spirit of Christ, which he revealed to the whole human race in his salvation mission. Life in the Holy Spirit of Christ is the opposite of existence in accord with human nature. Existence in accord with human nature is not life. Such existence is reactive and not proactive in the Holy Spirit of Christ. Pro-activity in the Holy Spirit of Christ is a gift of God. He means he is also the Holy Spirit, the Lord, the giver of life, the third person of the Trinity. There is no opposition in the Trinity. Harmony prevails between the three persons of the Trinity.

God has given us eternal life, and this life has its source in his Son. Whoever has the Son has this life; whoever does not have the Son of God does not have life. (1 John 5: 11-12)

But each one will be raised in the right order: Christ, first of all; then, at the time of his coming, those who belong to him. Then the end will come; Christ will overcome all spiritual rulers, authorities, and powers, and will hand over the Kingdom to God the Father. For Christ must rule until God defeats all enemies and puts them under his feet. The last enemy to be defeated will be death. (1 Cor 15: 23-26)

12. What does he mean by "no one"?

He means no person or being, seen and unseen. There is no exception or favour on account of sex, age, or status or on any ground.

13. What does he mean by "can come to the Father"?

"Can come" is referring to your soul coming to God for everlasting life after death and life after life. Christ is referring to sending your prayers to the Father. The Father means the Creator, the first person of the Trinity. To whom Christ will hand over the Kingdom at the end of the age.

14. What does Christ mean by "except through me"?

Christ means one can have everlasting life only through him. Christ is love. Love is God. Love comes only through Christ. Christ is referring to the Particular and Last Judgement through him, the King and the Judge. He is referring to himself as the second person of the Trinity. He is referring to salvation through his Church, the

Body of Christ. He is referring to salvation by his love, grace and gift. "Me" means the love of Christ for the whole human race.

15. What is the consequence of the declaration for ecumenism and unity of the Body of Christ?

Christ himself is shaping and directing ecumenism and unity in his Church. We all need to pray, and visibly come together day by day, as Christ prays for the unity of his Church and for the salvation of all the faithful. "I pray not only for these but also for those who through their teaching will come to believe in me. May they all be one, just as, Father, you are in me and I am in you, so that they also may be in us, so that the world may believe it was you who sent me. I have given them the glory you gave to me, that they may be one as we are one. With me in them and you in me, may they be so perfected in unity that the world will recognise that it was you who sent me and that you have loved them as you have loved me." (Jn 17: 20-23) JB

The declaration is a warning to both those who control the Church of Christ and all members who by conduct, action and inaction are dividing the body of Christ. The inheritance cannot be divided.

16. What is the consequence of the declaration for the Jews, Muslims, Hindus, Buddhists, Sikhs, other religions and atheists?

Will all these beautiful people created in the image and likeness of God go to hell outside the pale of salvation? No! Some will be saved by the grace of God and by their good deeds and charity even though they may not believe in God and Christ. God our Father is beneficent, merciful and forgiving.

The plan of salvation includes those who acknowledge the Creator, including the Muslims and the Jews. The Jews were the first to hear the Word of God. The Jews believe in one God as Christians. The Christian faith and the New Testament is the fulfilment of the Jewish faith and the Old Testament.

Muslims like Christians believe in one God. Muslims call God "Allah". Muslims believe in Jesus Christ as the messenger of God but not as the second person of the Trinity, God from God. But Muslims are still waiting to know the Most Holy Trinity, the Christian belief of one God in three persons: The Father, and the Son, and the Holy Spirit. Muslims profess to hold the faith of Abraham, and together with Christians they adore the one, merciful God, mankind's Judge on the last day.

God is experienced. Human intellect is too weak to understand God as he is Spirit. Faith in God is a gift. Salvation is a gift.

All the other religions claim to believe in God. Atheists believe in no God.

Who will be saved is only known to the Father through Christ. Human understanding is weak and cannot understand how the invisible God makes decisions.

17. What is the consequence of the declaration for lawyers, bankers, politicians, the media, the multinational corporations and other professional and vocational groups?

They should all repent and listen to the salvation message of Christ for renewal of their faith in the living God. They should live in accord with the Holy Spirit of Christ. He is forgiving. The risk is too big without Christ.

18. What shall we do to avoid going to hell?

Are you living your life in heaven or hell right now? When you die, are you going to heaven or hell? Practise life in the Holy Spirit of Jesus Christ. Keep the Commandments in its Spirit and not just its letter. Practise the sacraments. Pray to the Father through Christ. Worship the Creator and not the creation. Love one another in the Spirit of Christ, as Christ loves you, and you will have everlasting life.

God's Glory in Creation

How clearly the sky reveals God's glory!
How plainly it shows what he has done!
Each day announces it to the following day;
Each night repeats it to the next.
No speech or words are used, no sound is heard;
yet their message goes out to all the world
and is heard to the ends of the earth.

God made a home in the sky for the sun;
it comes out in the morning like a happy bridegroom,
like an athlete eager to run a race.
It starts at one end of the sky
and goes across to the other.
Nothing can hide from its heat.

The Law of the LORD is Perfect

The law of the LORD is perfect; it gives new strength.
The commands of the LORD are trustworthy,
giving wisdom to those who lack it.
The laws of the LORD are right,
and those who obey them are happy.
The commands of the LORD are just
And give understanding to the mind.
Reverence for the LORD is good;
it will continue for ever.
The judgements of the LORD are just;
they are always fair.
They are more desirable than the finest gold;
they are sweeter than the purest honey.
They give knowledge to me, your servant;
I am rewarded for obeying them.
No one can see his own errors;
deliver me, LORD, from hidden faults!
Keep me safe, also, from wilful sins;
don't let them rule over me.
Then I shall be perfect
and free from the evil of sin.
May my words and my thoughts be acceptable to you,
O LORD, my refuge and my redeemer! (Psalms 19)

Part Three

PRINCIPLES OF MANAGING INDUSTRY TRADE AND COMMERCE FOR REWARD WITH CONFIDENCE IN THE CONTEXT OF INSPIRATION BY THE HOLY SPIRIT

"But if any of you lack wisdom, you should pray to God, who will give it to you; because God gives generously and graciously to all. But when you pray, you must believe and not doubt at all." James 1: 5-6

"Each one of us has received a special gift in proportion to what Christ has given. It was he who "gave gifts"; he appointed some to be apostles, others to be prophets, others to be evangelists, others to be pastors and teachers. He did this to prepare all God's people for the work of Christian service, in order to build up the body of Christ" (Eph 4: 7, 11-12)

CHAPTER SIX

Principles of Managing Industry Trade and Commerce for Reward with Faith in God.

"You are worried and troubled over so many things, but just one thing is needed." Luke 10: 41-42

What is management? *The Lord's parable of the talents is instructive. *Faith in the living God is the cause and effect of the goals, vision and value of every human being. *Faith in the living God is the cause and effect of Wisdom for creativity endowed in our soul through Christ. *Faith in the living God is the cause and effect of effective communication endowed in our soul through Christ. *Faith in the living God is the cause and effect of time management endowed in our soul through Christ. *Absence of self-renewal through faith in Jesus Christ is the cause and effect of stress, which affects our health and life. *Faith in the living God is the cause and effect of responsibility and reward endowed in our soul through Christ. Just one thing is needed. *According to your faith, let it be unto you.

*What is Management?

Management means using certain skills or tools to make things happen in order to meet the value-driven goals of an enterprise in union with Christ. This means one must focus on one's own freely self-determined value-driven goals in union with Christ for reward and more responsibilities.

*The Lord's Parable of the Talents is instructive

Through the Lord's parable of the talents, Christ inaugurated economic freedom and free enterprise into the world in union with Christ. Christ recognises certain rights and liabilities under the Ten Commandments and the Lord's Sermon on the Mount in his inauguration for self-regulation.

Further implied rights and liabilities, which were recognised by Christ include the right of establishment in a foreign country, freedom from slavery, servitude or forced or compulsory labour, freedom of expression, freedom of assembly and association, freedom from discrimination, the right to property, the right to free elections, the right to international movement of persons and asylum seekers, the right to effective national and international remedy and the right to respect national and international authorities.

Through the wisdom of the parable of the talents, Christ asserts his authority over the whole creation. Christ appointed the whole human race as trustees and beneficiaries of the whole creation according to one's talent. Christ inaugurated free enterprise.

Every one is endowed by God with abilities for personal management of one's goals. This means one's endowment of the talents depends on one's standard of faith in the living God. This is empowerment for responsibilities according to one's faith in the living God through Christ.

Christ has given every trustee and beneficiary of the creation, abilities or talents for personal management of one's endowments to the glory of God through Christ. Every trustee is accountable for what is entrusted to him or her. Every trustee must be prepared to render accounts to Christ at any time an account is demanded by Christ.

Faithful discharge of the trust obligations endowed in one's soul through Christ means more responsibilities and happiness.

"At that time the Kingdom of heaven will be like this. Once there was a man who was about to go on a journey (*the man was the risen Lord Jesus Christ himself, God from God, Light from Light*); he called his servants (*the whole human race, who are made trustees and accountable to God through Christ and at the same time the beneficiaries of the heritage and the glory of God*) and put them in charge of his property (*dominion over all created things as trustees*). He gave to each one according to his ability (*the abilities are not equal*); to one he gave five thousand gold coins, to another he gave two thousand, and to another he gave one thousand. Then he left on his journey. [Italics mine.]

The servant who had received five thousand coins went at once and invested his money and earned another five thousand. In the same way the servant who had received two thousand coins earned another two thousand. But the servant who had received one thousand coins went off, dug a hole in the ground, and hid his master's money.

After a long time the master of those servants came back and settled accounts with them. The servant who had received five thousand coins came in and handed over the other five thousand. "You gave me five thousand coins, sir, he said. "Look! Here are another five thousand that I have earned." "Well done, you good and faithful servant!" said the master. "You have been faithful in managing small amounts, so I will put you in charge of large amounts. Come on in and share my happiness!"

Then the servant who had been given two thousand coins came in and said. "You gave me two thousand coins, sir. Look! Here are another two thousand that I have earned." "Well done, you good and faithful servant!" said his master. "You have been faithful in managing small amounts, so I will put you in charge of large amounts. Come on in and share my happiness!"

Then the servant who had received one thousand coins came in and said, "Sir, I know you are a hard man; you reap harvests where you did not sow, and you gather crops where you did not scatter seed. I was afraid, so I went off and hid your money in the ground. Look! Here is what belongs to you."

"You bad and lazy servant!" his master said. "You knew, did you, that I reap harvests where I did not sow, and gather crops where I did not sow, and gather crops where I did not scatter seed? Well, then, you should have deposited my money in the bank, and I would have received it all back with interest when I returned. Now, take the money away from him and give it to the one who has ten thousand coins.

For every person who has something (*faith in God*), even more will be given, and he will have more than enough; but the person who has nothing (*no faith in God*), even the little that he has will be taken away from him. [Italics mine].

As for this useless servant – throw him outside in the darkness; there he will cry and grind his teeth." *Mat 25: 14-30.*

***Faith in the living God is the cause and effect of the goals, vision and value of every human being.**

The first task of any enterprise is to determine its own goals or map in any trade, profession, vocation, employment or family. The goal or map tells the whole world where one is going.

The ability of the human being to freely determine or choose one's own goals or responsibilities and values in any trade, profession, vocation, employment or family in union with Christ is self- awareness or self-knowledge. The ability to make such a decision is leadership.

The most important task is to determine the value of the services and products of the enterprise. A value driven product or services will sell in any market irrespective of the climate and the weather.

Visualisation tool must be used to check the quality standard of the product or service. The product must be produced in the mind before it can be materialised.

The power of your goal is in Christ. The strength is in Christ. The goals must be realistic. The Holy Spirit will teach and guide you to make and achieve realistic goals.

The ability to determine your goals is within you. You must determine your goal your self. You must evaluate the goal your self. No one can determine and evaluate your goal for you. The goal must be value driven. That means it must be competitive in the market in terms of quality and price.

The opinion of the crowd may seek to overtake you, but stick to your own self determination of your goals and values. Others may help you to develop your goals. But they must help you in terms of your terms of reference and co-operate with you within your terms of reference.

Your conscience may help you. But your conscience may deceive you because it has not undergone the appropriate education, training and formation.

You must identify specific results to be achieved. This means you must clearly indicate what must be done, how to do it, and when to do it and who should do it. This is the responsibility of leadership.

You must identify the principles, which should be applied by management and employees in achieving the results of the enterprise. The guidelines for achieving the results of Jesus Christ in exploitation of the trusts and talents given to all human beings are set out in parts one to five of this book. Every one must undergo self-renewal and practise faith in the living God.

You must identify the human, financial, technical resources and organisational support you need to achieve the results. These are the infrastructure of the enterprise. They are the tools of the enterprise. The leadership of the enterprise must provide these resources and support in order to succeed in the enterprise.

In a state of self-renewal and self-knowledge, one can get access to these resources and support in union with Christ.

The enterprise must evaluate its goals. Evaluation means the enterprise must be able to know the good and bad fruits that it will reap as a result of the evaluation. If the evaluation is not good enough one should do further work and further evaluation for a better result.

You should be prepared to render accounts to members of the enterprise and the relevant authorities. Eventually you must be ready to render accounts to God through Christ. The teachings of Christ in this book will help you to render accounts to any one who demands accounts from you.

***Faith in the living God is the cause and effect of Wisdom for creativity endowed in our soul through Christ.**

Wisdom comes from within through Christ. Wisdom enables you to determine your own goals and materialise them.

Wisdom helps you to do visualisation, materialisation and marketing of your product and services.

Faith in the living God is the cause and effect of Wisdom. This means one must undergo regular self-renewal and self-knowledge exercise in order to meet the challenges of the creative process in union with Christ.

***Faith in the living God is the cause and effect of effective communication endowed in our soul through Christ.**

Communication is the most important management tool. Listening to understand, speaking, reading and writing are the four forms of communication commonly used in any enterprise or family. Listening to understand comes first.

The goal of listening to understand is to be able to understand another person's frame of reference. Understanding the map of another first enables you to get understanding of what the one is saying and where the one is coming from or going.

The prayer of St Francis of Assisi is instructive:

> "O Divine Master, grant that I may try
> not to be comforted, but to comfort;
> not to be understood, but to understand."

The key to good judgement is understanding. Understand first before what you said can be understood by the people of God, the customers, the clients and the workers.

***Faith in the living God is the cause and effect of time management endowed in our soul through Christ.**

Be always prepared because nobody knows the hour.

Time is important for self- renewal, education and training for self-knowledge. Devoting one hour every day to self-renewal and self-knowledge will produce a better result for the day than going without that devotion. That devotion restores your inherent tranquillity and enables you to use your time constructively.

Time is important but it cannot be stored in a bank as we do keep our money in a bank.

Time is important but we cannot buy it as we do buy any commodity in the market. So time is unique and we must use it wisely and constructively.

Time management is a habit and bad habit should be stopped and good habit should be encouraged.

The best approach is to identify clear goals and realistic objectives to be achieved from day to day. Respond to what is urgent first.

Delegate to others what you cannot cope with. But you remain as the principal and liable for the negligence of your agents or those to whom you have delegated your responsibilities.

Pressure of time can damage your health.

***Absence of self-renewal through faith in Jesus Christ is the cause and effect of stress, which affects our health and life.**

Stress is bad for our health. It does not permit us to enjoy life. Stress must be avoided at all costs. Prevention is better than cure. Self-renewal exercise helps to reduce stress.

The signs of stress include:

*Over eating. *Forgetfulness. *Excessive smoking. *Excessive worrying. *Fatigue. *Excessive alcohol. *Using sleeping pills. *Drugs. *Lack of appetite. *Indecisiveness. *Road rage driving. *Lack of humour. *Nausea. *Lack of relaxation. *Loss of concentration. *Inability to cope. *Indigestion. *Headaches. *Nail biting. *Sleeplessness. *Fainting. *Unreasonable sweating. *Desire to cry.*

Faith in the living God is the cause and effect of responsibility and reward endowed in our soul through Christ.

Inability to cope is due to lack of faith in God. This means one cannot respond to his trade, profession, vocation, employment and family responsibilities. The victim lacks response ability.

This is what happened to the person who was given one talent by Christ and because he was not able to cope he dug a hole in the ground and buried the talent.

The first remedy is to receive training and education in self-renewal and self-knowledge.

This book provides the solution.

Just One thing is needed

Just one thing is necessary for reconstruction and happiness. A fundamental principle of the market is that only what is needed by the consumer should be produced to meet the demand. This principle is taken to a higher plane in the Scriptures by our Lord Jesus Christ.

"As Jesus and his disciples went on their way, he came to a village where a woman named Martha welcomed him in her home. She had a sister named Mary, who sat down at the feet of the Lord and listened to his teaching. Martha was upset over all the work she had to do, so she came and said, "Lord, don't you care that my sister has left me to do all the work by myself? Tell her to come and help me!"

The Lord answered her, "Martha, Martha! You are worried and troubled over so many things, but just one is needed. Mary has chosen the right thing, and it will not be taken away from her." (Lk 10: 38-42)

What is needed is integration of our worldly interests (*Martha*) with our love of God and one another (*Mary*) and not one at the expense of the other. The body and the soul is one inseparable unity. After all the roundabouts, only love remains in the swing.

*According to your faith, let it be unto you.

Finally, every one will harvest whatever one sows in the Particular and the Last Judgement. Always be proactive. Never be reactive.

After all there is life after death for those who earn it in union with Christ. Seek first self-renewal in union with Christ and all other things will be added unto you.

Part Four

HUMAN FREEDOM IN THE HOLY SPIRIT OF JESUS CHRIST

"So then, submit to God. Resist the Devil, and he will run away from you." James 4: 7

CHAPTER SEVEN

Human Freedom in the Spirit of Jesus Christ

"I am the vine, and you are the branches. Those who remain in me, and I in them, will bear much fruit; for you can do nothing without me." Jn 15:5

1. Preserve your Salvation and Freedom from the Evil One. The Spirit and Human nature are enemies. The fruit of human nature. The Fruit of the Spirit. Bear one another's Burden. Judge your own conduct. Do not become tired of Doing Good: Sow and reap only in the Field of the Spirit. 2. No one can say "Jesus is Lord" without being informed by the Holy Spirit. 3. The Love of God and One Another. 4. The Lost Son, who Repented and Returned to his Father: Celebration of his Repentance.

1. Preserve your Salvation and Freedom from the Evil One

"Freedom is what we have – Christ has set us free! Stand, then, as free people, and do not allow yourselves to become slaves again. As for you my brothers and sisters, you were called to be free. But do not let this freedom become an excuse for letting your physical desires control you. Instead, let love make you serve one another. For the whole Law is summed up in one commandment: "Love your neighbour as you love yourself." But if you act like wild animals, hurting and harming each other, then watch out, or you will completely destroy one another."

The Spirit and Human Nature are Enemies

"What I say is this: let the Spirit direct your lives, and you will not satisfy the desires of the human nature. For what our human nature wants is opposed to what the Spirit wants, and what the Spirit wants is opposed to what our human nature wants. These two are enemies, and this means that you cannot do what you want to do. If the Spirit leads you, then you are not subject to the Law."

The Fruits of Human Nature

"What human nature does is quite plain. It shows itself in immoral, filthy, and indecent actions; in worship of idols and witchcraft. People become enemies and they fight; they become jealous, angry, and ambitious. They separate into parties and groups; they are envious, get drunk, have orgies, and do other things like these. I warn you now as I have before: those who do these things will not possess the Kingdom of God."

The Fruits of the Spirit

"But the Spirit produces love, joy, peace, patience, kindness, goodness, faithfulness, humility, and self-control. There is no law against such things as these. And those who belong to Christ Jesus have put to death their human nature with all its passions and desires. The Spirit has given us life; he must also control our lives. We must not be proud or irritate one another or be jealous of one another."

Bear one another's Burdens

"My brothers and sisters, if someone is caught in any kind of wrong-doing, those of you who are spiritual should set him right; but you must do it in a gentle way. And keep an eye on yourselves, so that you will not be tempted, too. Help to carry one another's burdens, and in this way you will obey the law of Christ."

Judge your own Conduct

"If someone thinks he or she is somebody when really they are nobody, they are only deceiving themselves. You should each judge your own conduct. If it is good, then you can be proud of what you yourself have done, without having to compare it with what someone else has done. For we each have our own load to carry."

Do not become tired of doing Good: Sow and Reap only in the Field of the Spirit

"Those who are being taught the Christian message should share all the good things they have with their teachers.

Do not deceive yourselves; no one makes a fool of God. People will reap exactly what they sow. If they sow in the field of their natural desires, from it they will gather the harvest of death; if they sow in the field of the Spirit, from the Spirit they will gather the harvest of eternal life.

So let us not become tired of doing good; for if we do not give up, the time will come when we will reap the harvest. So then, as often as we have the chance, we should do good to everyone, and especially to those who belong to our family in the faith." *Gal 5: 1, 13-26; 6: 1-10*

2. No one can say "Jesus is Lord" without being informed by the Holy Spirit. *1 Cor 12:*

"I am the way, the truth and the life; no one goes to the Father except by me." *Jn 14: 6.*

"When you lift up the Son of Man, you will know that "I Am Who I Am; then you will know that I do nothing on my own authority, but I say only what the Father has instructed me to say. And he who sent me is with me; he has not left me alone, because I always do what pleases him, Many who heard Jesus say these things believed in him. So Jesus said to those who believed in him, "If you obey my teachings, you are really my disciples; you will know the truth, and the truth will set you free." *Jn 8: 28-32.*

"Do you not believe, Philip, that I am in the Father and the Father is in me? The words that I have spoken to you, Jesus said to his disciples, do not come from me. The Father, who remains in me, does his own work. Believe me when I say that I am in the Father and the Father is in me. If not, believe because of the things I do. I am telling you the truth: those who believe in me will do what I do – yes, they will do even greater things, because I am going to the Father. And I will do whatever you ask for in my name, so that the Father's glory will be shown through the Son. If you ask me for anything in my name, I will do it." *Jn 14: 10-14.*

"I am the bread of life, Jesus told them. Those who come to me will never be hungry; those who believe in me will never be thirsty. Now, I told you that you have seen me but will not believe. Everyone whom my Father gives me will come to me. I will never turn away anyone who comes to me, because I have come down from heaven to do not my own will but the will of him who sent me. And it is the will of him who sent me that I should not lose any of all those he has given me, but that I should raise them all to life on the last day. For what my Father wants is that all who see the Son and believe in him should have eternal life. And I will raise them to life on the last day." *Jn 6: 35-40.*

"Do not believe me, then, if I am not doing the things my Father wants me to do. But if I do them, even though you do not believe me, you should at least believe my deeds, in order that you may know once and for all that the Father is in me and that I am in the Father." *Jn 10: 37-38.*

"I am telling you the truth: I am the gate for the sheep. All others who came before me are thieves and robbers, but the sheep did not listen to them. I am the gate. Whoever comes in by me will be saved; they will come in and go out and find pastures. The thief comes only in order to steal, kill, and destroy. I have come in order that you might have life – life in its fullness. I am the good shepherd, who is willing to die for the sheep." *Jn 10: 7-11.*

"Yes, said Jesus, if you yourself can (*have faith in me*)! Everything is possible by faith." *Mark 9: 23.* [*Italics mine*]

"Come, whoever is thirsty; accept the water of life as a gift, whoever wants it." *Rev 22: 17.* "To anyone who is thirsty I will give the right to drink from the spring of the water of life without paying for it." *Rev 21: 6.* "Whoever is thirsty should come to me, and whoever believes in me should drink." *Jn 7: 37-38.*

3. The Love of God and One Another

"For God so loved the world that he gave his only Son that whoever believes in him should not perish, but have eternal life." *Jn 3: 16.*

"This hope does not disappoint us, for God has poured out his love into our hearts by means of the Holy Spirit, who is God's gift to us. For when we were still helpless, Christ died for the wicked at the time that God chose. It is a difficult thing for someone to die for a righteous person. It may even be that someone might dare to die for a good person. But God has shown us how much he loves us - it was while we were still sinners that Christ died for us! By his blood we are now put right with God." *Rom 5: 5-9.*

"I come so that they may have life and have it in abundance." *Jn 10:10.* "And now I give you a new commandment: love one another. As I have loved you, so you must love one another." *Jn 13: 34.*

"My commandment is this: love one another, just as I love you. The greatest love a person can have for his friends is to give his life for them." *Jn 15: 12-13.*

"But when the kindness and love of God our Saviour was revealed, he saved us. It was not because of any good deeds that we ourselves had done, but because of his own mercy that he saved us, through the Holy Spirit, who gives us new birth and new life by washing us. God poured out the Holy Spirit abundantly on us through Jesus Christ our Saviour, so that by his grace we might be put right with God and come into possession of the eternal life we hope for. This is a true saying." *Titus 3: 4-8.*

"If you love me, you will obey my commandments. I will ask the Father, and he will give you another Helper, who will stay with you forever. He is the Spirit who reveals the truth about God. The world cannot receive him, because it cannot see him or know him. But you know him, because he remains with you and is in you." *Jn 14: 15-1.*

"Whoever loves me will obey my teaching. My Father will love him, and my Father and I will come to him and live with him." *Jn 14:23.*

"Those who accept my commandments and obey them are the ones who love me. My Father will love those who love me; I too will love them and reveal myself to them." *Jn 14: 21.*

"I chose you and appointed you to go and bear much fruit, the kind of fruit that endures. And so the Father will give you whatever you ask of him in my name. This, then is what I command you: love one another." *Jn 15: 16-17.*

"So get rid of your old self, which made you live as you used to – the old self that was being destroyed by its deceitful desires. Your hearts and minds must be made completely new, and you must put on the new self, which is created in God's likeness and reveals itself in the true life that is upright and holy.

No more lying, then! Each of you must tell the truth to one another, because we are all members together in the body of Christ. If you become angry, do not let your anger lead you into sin, and do not stay angry all day. Don't give the Devil a chance. Those who used to rob must stop robbing and start working, in order to earn an honest living for themselves and to be able to help the poor. Do not use harmful words, but only helpful words, the kind that build up and provide what is needed, so that what you say will do good to those who hear you. And do not make God's Holy Spirit sad; for the Spirit is God's mark of ownership on you, a guarantee that the Day will come when God will set you free. Get rid of all bitterness, passion, and anger. No more shouting or insults, no more hateful feelings of any sort. Instead, be kind and tender-hearted to one another, and forgive one another, as God has forgiven you through Christ." *Eph 4: 22-32.*

To love God and one another means we must obey and practise the whole Law of God. The will of God is what is good and perfect before God. Let us do the will of God by loving God and one another.

4. The Lost Son, who Repented and Returned to his Father: Celebration of his Repentance.

"Jesus went on to say, "There was once a man who had two sons. The younger one said to him, "Father, give me my share of the property now." So the man divided his property between his two sons.

After a few days the younger son sold his part of the property and left home with the money. He went to a country far away, where he wasted his money in reckless living. He spent everything he had.

Then a severe famine spread over that country, and he was left without a thing. So he went to work for one of the citizens of that country, who sent him out to his farm to take care of the pigs. He wished he could fill himself with the bean pods the pigs ate, but no one gave him anything to eat.

At last he came to his senses and said, "All my father's hired workers have more than they can eat, and here I am about to starve! I will get up and go to my father and say, Father, I have sinned against God and against you. I am no longer fit to be called your son; treat me as one of your hired workers." So he got up and started back to his father.

He was still a long way from home when his father saw him; his heart was filled with pity, and he ran, threw his arms round his son, and kissed him.

"Father," the son said, "I have sinned against God and against you. I am no longer fit to be called your son." But the father called his servants. "Hurry!" he said. "Bring the best robe and put it on him. Put a ring on his finger and shoes on his feet. Then go and get the prize calf and kill it, and let us celebrate with a feast! For this son of mine was dead, but now he is alive; he was lost, but now he has been found." And so the feasting began.

In the mean time the elder son was out in the field. On his way back, when he came close to the house, he heard music and dancing. So he called one of the servants and asked him, "what's going on?" "Your brother has come back home," the servant answered, "and your father has killed the prize calf, because he got him back safe and sound."

The elder brother was so angry that he would not go into the house; so his father came out and begged him to come in. But he answered his father, "Look, all these years I have worked for you like a slave, and I have never disobeyed your orders. What have you given me? Not even a goat for me to have a feast with my friends But this son of yours wasted all your property on prostitutes, and when he comes back home, you kill the prize calf for him!

"My son, the father answered, "you are always here with me, and everything I have is yours. But we had to celebrate and be happy, because your brother was dead, but now he is alive; he was lost, but now he has been found" *Lk 15: 11-32.*

CHAPTER EIGHT

The Lord's Sermon on the Mount for Self-Renewal

"If you obey my teaching, you are really my disciples; you will know the truth, and the truth will set you free." Jn 8: 31-32

True Happiness. You are the salt for transforming the whole human race. You are the light for the whole human race. Teaching about the Law and fulfilment of the Law. Teaching about anger: the new standard higher than the old. Teaching about adultery: the new standard higher than the old. Teaching about divorce: the new standard higher than the old. Teaching about wows: the new standard higher than the old. Teaching about revenge: the new standard higher than the old. Love of Enemies: the new standard higher than the old. Teaching about charity: almsgiving in secret. Teaching about Prayer: Prayer in secret. How to Pray. The Lord's Prayer. Teaching about Fasting: Fasting in secret. Riches in heaven: True treasures. The eye, the lamp of the body. Possessions: Trust only the invisible true God. Do not judge others. Do not profane sacred things. Ask, Seek, Knock: Effective Prayer. The golden rule. The narrow and wide gate: Do not follow the Crowd but follow only Christ. A tree and its fruits: Know the False Prophets by the Quality of their Life and Fruits. Be the true disciple of Christ else I will say to you I never Knew you. The true disciple of Christ builds on a Rock. The false disciple builds in Sand. The Authority of Jesus Christ.

"Jesus saw the crowds and went up a hill, where he sat down. His disciples gathered round him, and he began to teach them:

True Happiness

Happy are those who know they are spiritually poor; the Kingdom of heaven belongs to them!
Happy are those who mourn; God will comfort them!

Happy are those who are humble; they will receive what God has promised!
Happy are those whose greatest desire is to do what God requires; God will satisfy them fully!
Happy are those who are merciful to others; God will be merciful to them!
Happy are the pure in heart; they will see God!
Happy are those who work for peace; God will call them his children!
Happy are those who are persecuted because they do what God requires; the Kingdom of heaven belongs to them!
Happy are you when people insult you and persecute you and tell all kinds of evil lies against you because you are my followers. Be happy and glad, for a great reward is kept for you in heaven. This is how the prophets who lived before you were persecuted.

You are the salt for transforming the whole human race

You are like salt for the whole human race. But if salt loses its saltiness, there is no way to make it salty again. It has become worthless, so it is thrown out and people trample on it.

You are the light for the whole human race

You are like light for the whole world. A city built on a hill cannot be hidden. No one lights a lamp and puts it under a bowl; instead he puts it on the lamp stand, where it gives light for everyone in the house. In the same way your light must shine before people, so that they will see the good things you do and praise your Father in heaven.

Teaching about the Law and fulfilment of the Law

Do not think that I have come to do away with the Law of Moses and the teachings of the prophets. I have not come to do away with them, but to make their teachings come true. Remember that as long as heaven and earth last, not the least point nor the smallest detail of the Law will be done away with – not until the end of all things. So then, whoever disobeys even the least important of the commandments and teaches others to do the same, will be least in the Kingdom of heaven. On the other hand, whoever obeys the Law and teaches others to do the same, will be great in the Kingdom of heaven. I tell you, then, that you will be able to enter the Kingdom of heaven only if you are more faithful than the teachers of the Law and the Pharisees in doing what God requires.

Teaching about Anger: the new standard higher than the old

You have heard that people were told in the past, "Do not commit murder; anyone who does will be brought to trial." But now I tell you: whoever is angry with his brother will be brought to trial, whoever calls his brother "You good-for-nothing!" will be brought before the Council, and whoever calls his brother a worthless fool will be in danger of going to the fire of hell. So if you are about to offer your gift to God at the altar and there you remember that your brother has something against you, leave your gift there in front of the altar, go at once and make peace with your brother, and then come back and offer your gift to God.

If someone brings a lawsuit against you and takes you to court, settle the dispute with him while there is time, before you get to court. Once you are there, he will hand you over to the judge, who will hand you over to the police, and you will be put in jail. There you will stay, I tell you, until you pay the last penny of your fine.

Teaching about Adultery: the new standard higher than the old

You have heard that it was said, "Do not commit adultery." But now I tell you: anyone who looks at a woman and wants to possess her is guilty of committing adultery with her in his heart. So if your right eye causes you to sin, take it out and throw it away! It is much better for you to lose a part of your body than to have your whole body thrown into hell. If your right hand causes you to sin, cut it off and throw it away! It is much better for you to lose one of your limbs than for your whole body to go to hell.

Teaching about Divorce: the new standard higher than the old

It was also said, "Anyone who divorces his wife must give her a written notice of divorce." But now I tell you: if a man divorces his wife, for any cause other than her unfaithfulness, then he is guilty of making her commit adultery if she marries again; and the man who marries her commits adultery also.

Teaching about Vows: the new standard higher than the old

You have also heard that people were told in the past, "Do not break your promise, but do what you have vowed to the Lord to do." But I tell you: do not use any vow when you make a promise. Do not swear by heaven, for it is God's throne; nor by earth, for it is the resting place for his feet; nor by Jerusalem, for it is the city of the great King. Do not even swear by your head, because you cannot make a single hair white or black. Just say "Yes" or "No" – anything else you say comes from the Evil One.

Teaching about Revenge: and Non-resistance: the new standard higher than the old

You have heard that it was said, "An eye for an eye, and a tooth for a tooth." But now I tell you: do not take revenge on someone who wrongs you. If anyone slaps you on the right cheek, let him slap your left cheek too. And if someone takes you to court to sue you for your shirt, let him have your coat as well. And if one of the occupation troops forces you to carry his pack one kilometre, carry it two kilometres. When someone asks you for something, give it to him; when someone wants to borrow something, lend it to him.

Love Your Enemies: the new standard higher than the old

You have heard that it was said, "Love your friends, hate your enemies." But now I tell you: love your enemies and pray for those who persecute you, so that you may become the children of your Father in heaven. For he makes his sun to shine on bad and good people alike, and gives rain to those who do good and those who do evil. Why should God reward you if you love only the people who love you? Even the tax collectors do that! And if you speak only to your friends, have you done anything out of the ordinary? Even the pagans do that! You must be perfect – just as your Father in heaven is perfect!

Teaching about Charity: Almsgiving in secret

Make certain you do not perform your religious duties in public so that people will see what you do. If you do these things publicly, you will not have any reward from your Father in heaven.

So when you give something to a needy person, do not make a big show of it, as the hypocrites do in the houses of worship and on the streets. They do it so that people will praise them. I assure you, they have already been paid in full. But when you help a needy person, do it in such a way that even your closest friend will not know about it. Then it will be a private matter. And your Father, who sees what you do in private, will reward you.

Teaching about Prayer: Prayer in secret

When you pray, do not be like the hypocrites! They love to stand up and pray in the houses of worship and on the street corners, so that everyone will see them. I assure you, they have already been paid in full. But when you pray, go to your room, close the door, and pray to your Father, who is unseen. And your Father, who sees what you do in private, will reward you.

How to pray. The Lord's Prayer

When you pray, do not use a lot of meaningless words, as the pagans do, who think that their gods will hear them because their prayers are long. Do not be like them. Your Father already knows what you need before you ask him. This, then, is how you should pray:

"Our Father in heaven:
May your holy name be honoured;
may your Kingdom come;
may your will be done on earth as it is in heaven.
Give us today the food we need.
Forgive us the wrongs we have done,
as we forgive the wrongs that others have done to us.
Do not bring us to hard testing,
But keep us safe from the Evil One."

If you forgive others the wrongs they have done to you, your Father in heaven will also forgive you. But if you do not forgive others, then your Father will not forgive the wrongs you have done.

Teaching about Fasting: Fasting in secret

And when you fast, do not put on a sad face as the hypocrites do. They neglect their appearance so that everyone will see that they are fasting. I assure you, they have already been paid in full. When you go without food, wash your face and comb your hair, so that others cannot know that you are fasting— only your Father, who is unseen, will know. And your Father, who sees what you do in private, will reward you.

Riches in Heaven. True treasures

Do not store up riches for yourselves here on earth, where moths and rust destroy, and robbers break in and steal. Instead, store up riches for yourselves in heaven, where moths and rust cannot destroy, and robbers cannot break in and steal. For your heart will always be where your riches are.

The eye, the Lamp of the Body

The eyes are like a lamp for the body. If your eyes are sound, your whole body will be full of light; but if your eyes are no good, your body will be darkness. So if the light in you is darkness, how terribly dark it will be!

Possessions: Trust only the Invisible true God

No one can be a slave of two masters; he will hate one and love the other; he will be loyal to one and despise the other. You cannot serve both God and money.

This is why I tell you not to be worried about the food and drink you need in order to stay alive, or about clothes for your body. After all, isn't life worth more than food? And isn't the body worth more than clothes? Look at the birds: they do not sow seeds, gather a harvest and put it in barns; yet your Father in heaven takes care of them! Aren't you worth much more than birds? Can any of you live a bit longer by worrying about it?

And why worry about clothes? Look how the wild flowers grow: they do not work or make clothes for themselves. But I tell you that not even King Solomon with all his wealth had clothes as beautiful as one of these flowers. It is God who clothes the wild grass – grass that is here today and gone tomorrow, burnt up in the oven. Won't he be all the more sure to clothe you? How little faith you have!

So do not start worrying: Where will my food come from ? or my drink? or my clothes? (These are the things the pagans are always concerned about.) Your Father in heaven knows that you need all these things. Instead, be concerned above everything else with the Kingdom of God and with what he requires of you, and he will provide you with all these other things.

So do not worry about tomorrow; it will have enough worries of its own. There is no need to add to the troubles each day brings.

Do not Judge others

Do not judge others, so that God will not judge you, for God will judge you in the same way as you judge others, and he will apply to you the same rules you apply to others. Why, then, do you look at the speck in your brother's eye, and pay no attention to the log in your own eye? How dare you say to your brother, Please, let me take that speck out of your eye," when you have a log in your own eye? You hypocrite! First take the log out of your own eye, and then you will be able to see clearly to take the speck out of your brother's eye.

Do not profane sacred things

Do not give what is holy to dogs – they will only turn and attack you. Do not throw your pearl in front of pigs – they will only trample them underfoot.

Ask Seek, Knock: Effective prayer

Ask. And you will receive; seek, and you will find; knock, and the door will be opened to you. For everyone who asks will receive, and anyone who seeks will find, and the door will be opened to those who knock. Would any of you who are fathers give your son a stone when he asks for bread? Or would you give him a snake when he asks for a fish? Bad as you are, you know how to give good things to your children. How much more, then, will your Father in heaven give good things to those who ask him!

The golden rule

Do for others what you want them to do for you: this is the meaning of the Law of Moses and of the teachings of the prophets.

The Narrow and Wide Gate. Do not Follow the Crowd but Follow only Christ

Go in through the narrow gate, because the gate to hell is wide and the road that leads to it is easy, and there are many who travel it. But the gate to life is narrow and the way that leads to it is hard, and there are few people who find it.

A Tree and its Fruit: Know the False Prophets by the Quality of their Life and Fruit

Be on your guard against false prophets; they come to you looking like sheep on the outside, but on the inside they are really like wild wolves. You will know them by what they do. Thorn bushes do not bear grapes, and briars do not bear figs. A healthy tree bears good fruit, but a poor tree bears bad fruit. A healthy tree cannot bear bad fruit, and a poor tree cannot bear good fruit. And any tree that does not bear good fruit is cut down and thrown in the fire. So then, you will know the false prophets by what they do.

Be the true disciple of Christ else I will say to you I Never Knew You

Not everyone who calls me "Lord, Lord" will enter the Kingdom of heaven, but only those who do what my Father in heaven wants them to do. When Judgement Day comes, many will say to me, "Lord, Lord! In your name we spoke God's message, by your name we drove out many demons and performed many miracles! Then I will say to them, "I never knew you. Get away from me, you wicked people!"

The True Disciple of Christ Builds on rock

So then, anyone who hears these words of mine and obeys them is like a wise man who built his house on rock. The rain poured down, the rivers overflowed, and the wind blew hard against that house. But it did not fall, because it was built on rock.

The False Disciple Builds on sand

But anyone who hears these words of mine and does not obey them is like a foolish man who built his house on sand. The rain poured down, the rivers overflowed, the wind blew hard against that house, and it fell. And what a terrible fall that was!

The Authority of Jesus Christ

When Jesus finished saying these things, the crowd was amazed at the way he taught. He wasn't like the teachers of the Law: instead, he taught with authority." *Matt 5-7.* [*Some sub-headings mine*].

CHAPTER NINE

The Ten Commandments for Self-renewal in the context of human rights

"If you love me, you will obey my commandments I will ask the Father, and he will give you another Helper, who will stay with you for ever. He is the Spirit who reveals the truth about God" Jn 14:15-17

The Biblical Version of the Ten Commandments. The short version of the Ten Commandments. Application of the Ten Commandments for self-renewal. Reducing the Ten Commandments into two Commandments based on Love. Who is my neighbour? The good Samaritan response. What are the human rights in the Ten Commandments for Reconstruction and Happiness?

The Biblical version of the Ten Commandments

"God spoke, and these were his words: I am the LORD your God who brought you out of Egypt, where you were slaves.

Worship no god but me.

Do not make for yourselves images of anything in heaven or on earth or in the water under the earth. Do not bow down to any idol or worship it, because I am the LORD your God and I tolerate no rivals. I bring punishment on those who hate me and on their descendants down to the third and fourth generation. But I show my love to thousands of generations of those who love me and obey my laws.

Do not use my name for evil purposes, for I, the LORD your God, will punish anyone who misuses my name.

Observe the Sabbath and keep it holy. You have six days in which to do your work, but the seventh day is a day of rest dedicated to me. On that day no one is to work – neither you, your children, your slaves, your animals, nor the foreigners who live in your country. In six days I, the LORD, made the earth, the sky, the sea, and everything in them, but on the seventh day I rested. That is why I, the LORD, blessed the Sabbath and made it holy.

Respect your father and your mother, so that you may live a long time in the land that I am giving you.

Do not commit adultery.

Do not steal.

Do not accuse anyone falsely.

Do not desire another man's house; do not desire his wife, his slaves, his cattle, his donkeys, or anything else that he owns." Amen. *Exd 20: 1-17; Deut 5: 6-21.*

The short version of the Ten Commandments

I am the Lord your God. Do not have other gods before me.
Do not use the name of the LORD your God in vain.
Remember the Sabbath day.
Honour your father and mother.
Do not kill.
Do not commit murder
Do not commit adultery.
Do not steal.
Do not give false witness against your neighbour.
Do not covet your neighbour's wife.
Do not covet your neighbour's goods.

Application of the Ten Commandments for Self-Renewal

I am the Lord your God. Do not have other gods before me.
This prohibition includes Satanic worship and all indigenous and self-invented African worships, eg vodoo, yewe, afa, torgbe-zikpui, tror, practices of mediums, dzudzu worship, idols and neglect to worship the invisible living God only. These Africans could not respond to the living God. They lacked response abilities.

These African worships contributed to the poor condition of life on the Continent; but the practices have almost disappeared in the light of general education and Christianity. The truth of Christ has set Africa and the whole human race free from the Evil One and his discredited tricks and ignorance.

Do not use the name of the Lord your God in vain.
This prohibition includes mocking God, seriously cursing the invisible God and blaming God for the consequences of worshipping idols and other created things instead of the Creator.

Remember to keep holy the Sabbath day.
Working on Sundays and ignoring rest and prayer. Missing Sunday Mass and Mass on Holy Days of Obligation, e.g. the Feast of the Epiphany without reason. But you can save life on Sunday because that is in harmony with the will of the invisible God, the Creator of life.

Honour your father and mother.
This command implies the right to marry and found a family; the right to respect for private and family life, home and correspondence and the right to procreation and education of children.

This command imposes a duty of care to respect parents' advice, which is consistent with the spirit of the Ten Commandments. Sons and daughters owe a duty to provide financial assistance to their parents in old age and provide for their burial. Parents must be visited at old age and they should not be neglected in any way.

Do not kill.
This prohibition includes right to life, abortion, suicide, mercy killing, killing in the course of anger, unjustified killing and heavy and persistent alcoholic drinking leading to death and torture or inhuman or degrading treatment or punishment leading to death. This command may include killing in the course of any unreasonable war or emergency declared by any group or government.

Do not commit adultery.
Desiring another person's spouse by thought. Trial marriages. Homosexual conduct.

Do not steal.
This prohibition includes deprivation of another person of what belongs to him without real consent whilst that person is in need of the property.

Laziness at work and taking wages without offering adequate services for it.

Taking your employer's goods left in your care by your employer for use at home or to sell to another. Shop-lifting.

Do not give false witness against your neighbour.
This prohibition includes going to court to stand as a witness for someone or your self knowing well that your statement is not true. This prohibition implies the right to liberty, freedom from torture or inhuman or degrading treatment or punishment, security of the person and the right to a fair trial.

You shall not covet your neighbour's wife.
This prohibition includes any sexual act forbidden under the Sixth Commandment.

Do not covet your neighbour's goods.
This prohibition includes uncontrolled desire for another person's goods. This includes receiving stolen property or buying it from the thief. Taking another person's property without real and informed consent of the owner.

Reducing the Ten Commandments into two Commandments based on Unconditional Love of one another.

A teacher of the Law asked Jesus: Which commandment is the most important of all?" "Jesus replied, "The most important one is this: Listen, Israel! The Lord our God is the only Lord. Love the Lord your God with all your heart, with all your soul, with all your mind, and with all your strength. The second most important commandment is this: Love your neighbour as you love yourself. There is no other commandment more important than these two." *Mk 12: 29-31.*

Who is my neighbour? The parable of the good Samaritan Response.

"A teacher of the Law came up and tried to trap Jesus. "Teacher," he asked, "what must I do to receive eternal life?" Jesus answered him, "What do the Scriptures say? How do you interpret them?" The man answered, "Love the Lord your God with all your heart, with all your soul, with all your strength, and with all your mind; and love your neighbour as you love yourself."

You are right, Jesus replied; do this and you will live. But the teacher of the Law wanted to justify himself, so he asked Jesus, "Who is my neighbour?"

Jesus answered, There was once a man who was going down from

Jerusalem to Jericho when robbers attacked him, stripped him, and beat him up, leaving him half dead. It so happened that a priest was going down that road; but when he saw the man, he walked on by, on the other side. In the same way a Levite also came along, went over and looked at the man, and then walked on by, on the other side. But a Samaritan who was travelling that way came upon the man, and when he saw him, his heart was filled with pity. He went over to him, poured oil and wine on his wounds and bandaged them; then he put the man on his own animal and took him to an inn, where he took care of him. The next day he took out two silver coins and gave them to the innkeeper. Take care of him, he told the innkeeper, and when I come back this way, I will pay you whatever else you spend on him.

And Jesus concluded, in your opinion, which one of these three acted like a neighbour towards the man attacked by the robbers?

The teacher of the Law answered, *the one who was kind to him.* Jesus replied, *you go, then, and do the same.*" *Lk 10: 25-37.*

What are the human rights in the Ten Commandments for Reconstruction and Happiness?

Human rights are inherent in the Ten Commandments expressly or by implication. The purpose of this sub-heading is to summarise some of these human rights in order to inform and clarify the mind. The Good News is for protecting the fundamental human rights of the people for reconstruction and happiness worldwide.

Human rights are fundamental rights inherent in every human being created in the image and likeness of God. One person's right is another person 's duty. There is no right without a corresponding duty.

The emergence of the sovereign state, which claims every right and control over the life of its subjects means that it must also have the corresponding duty to protect the fundamental human rights of its subjects and be liable for breach of these fundamental rights within its jurisdiction.

Some human rights are absolute and some are qualified rights. Some are protected in international law or national law or both or not in national law at all. In some countries only qualified human rights are protected. Some countries refuse to recognise even the absolute human rights like the right to life. In brief, whether one enjoys human rights or not depends on the country in which one resides.

Generally, it is the sovereign state, which breaches the human rights of its citizens and inhabitants because of its capacity to abuse its sovereignty and its people. But powerful companies and individuals do also infringe human rights of people. In any case the sovereign state is liable for breach of human rights within its jurisdiction on the ground that those companies and individuals are under the control of the sovereign state.

The issue of human rights is important because denial of human rights affects reconstruction, development and the quality of life of people in any country. Every one is entitled to life before death.

Human rights include the absolute right to life, right of access to safe water and sanitary means of waste disposal, right to peace, right to health, right to facility for treatment, right to food, right to shelter, right to clothes, freedom from the death or execution penalty, freedom from torture, inhuman or degrading treatment or punishment, freedom from slavery, servitude or forced or compulsory labour, right to liberty and integrity and security of person, right to a fair trial, freedom from retroactive criminal offences, right to respect for private and family life, home and correspondence, freedom of religion, thought and conscience, freedom of expression and communication, freedom of assembly and association, right to marry and found a family, right to effective domestic human rights remedy, freedom from discrimination in respect of protected rights, derogation from human rights in time of war or other public emergency, right to own property, right to work, right to equal pay and minimum wages, right to trade, right to finance, right to vote, right to education, right to election, freedom from imprisonment for non-fulfilment of contractual obligation, freedom of movement within a state and to leave its territory for another territory, right of a national not to be expelled from and to enter a state 's territory, freedom of aliens from collective expulsion, freedom of expulsion of individual aliens, right to review on appeal in criminal cases, right to compensation for miscarriage of justice, freedom from double jeopardy or being tried twice for the same offence, equality of the right of spouse, right to peaceful settlement of industrial dispute, right to strike as a last resort, right of a child to protection, right to complain against public authorities and right to equality and non-discrimination. Categories of human rights are not closed.

Human rights are protected under the Ten Commandments as clarified and supplemented by the Lord 's Sermon on the Mount. The basic rule of Christianity, which enforces human rights worldwide was proclaimed by Jesus Christ himself when he said: "Love one another just as I love you."

According to the Encyclopaedia Britannica, Christianity has 2 billion followers out of 5.8 billion of the world population. Muslims have 971,507,000 adherents. The Muslims were followed by Hindus, Buddhists, Atheists, Sikhs, Jews and other faiths. .(See Table of Adherents of all faiths in the introduction Chapter of this book.)

The truth of the matter is that not all followers of these faith groups practise their faith or are human rights compliant. Let alone the sovereign state. All of them must seek freedom from servitude to sin and death for reconstruction and development worldwide.

In any event respect for human freedom is vital for reconstruction and improvement in quality of life worldwide. Disrespect of human rights is a barrier to international capital investment and trade. Lack of human rights increases the risk of the return of capital and profit to the investors and the investees. The result in that circumstance is negative investment and reconstruction.

Part Five

PRAYER AND THE GRACE OF THE SACRAMENTS FOR SELF-RENEWAL

"I tell you: when you pray and ask for something, believe that you have received it, and you will be given whatever you ask for." Mark 11: 24

CHAPTER TEN

Prayer in the Life of the whole human race for Self-Renewal

"God is Spirit, and only by the power of his Spirit can people worship him as he really is" Jn 4:24

What is prayer? Adoration. Blessing. Meditation. Contemplation. Vocal prayer. How do we know whether what we are doing is prayer to God? The Christian Liturgy. Where should the liturgy be celebrated. The Lord's Prayer. The Lord is my Shepherd. The Hail Mary. Hail Holy Queen. The Prayer of St Francis of Assisi. The Glory be. Prayer for the Dead. An Act of Love of God and Neighbour. Prayer is answered in a state of humility and freedom from the world. Warning against Judging another person and a Fellow-Christian. Warning for the Rich and the Over-confident person. The Parable of the Widow and the Judge.

What is Prayer?

Through the Word of God in the Scriptures, God first speaks in prayer revealing his mysteries and secret of love to all human beings through Christ. All human beings must speak in prayer in a state of stillness and attention in answer to God for the grace of God. Prayer is thinking the thoughts of God.

Prayer is the spiritual energy being released in the presence of the living God in the name of the risen Lord Jesus Christ to enable one to receive the gifts of the Holy Spirit through Christ. Prayer is the most powerful spiritual weapon for victory over temptation and the Evil One, who opposes our salvation through Christ. Prayer is an invitation to the Holy Spirit to abide in us through Christ.

Through mental words in meditation or contemplation or vocal words in a vocal prayer, a Christian prayer to God, if true from the heart, like the prayer of the sinner tax collector of the Gospel, achieves response and union with the prayer of the risen Lord Jesus Christ.

Every prayer will be answered if it is based on a firm faith and belief in the risen Lord Jesus Christ. Faith in the risen Lord means compliance with the Law of the Holy Spirit. The Law of the Holy Spirit is the Law of the Gospel and the Ten Commandments as interpreted and fulfilled by the risen Lord in the Lord's Sermon on the Mount.

Prayer is a battle in stillness and attentiveness in the Kingdom of God within every human being. Every one must fight and win his or her battle for salvation through the grace of the risen Lord Jesus Christ. Prayer is like a mustard seed, which with care, patience, hope and attention, will grow in you and will become a refuge for salvation for all seasons in union with Christ.

Prayer is the common word for all our supplications, meditation, contemplation and vocal prayer. The way in which a prayer is said makes one to give it different names. If the prayer is true, all will be answered by Almighty God and all souls will be saved from sin, death and the Evil One through the grace of the risen Lord Jesus Christ, irrespective of the way it is expressed.

Adoration

Adoration is the first stage of prayer in the presence of God. The faithful acknowledges the holy name of God as he is. Once the faithful is grasped by the unity and the love of his holy name, adoration begins. Adoration is the first response of the faithful to God acknowledging the lowly status of the faithful in the presence of the almighty God, the Creator of heaven and earth, the source of all gifts. This adoration and exaltation of the invisible God in respectful silence, humility and total faith in the living God guarantees the acceptance of the supplications of the faithful by the Father through Christ. "For all who make themselves great will be humbled, and all who humble themselves will be made great."

We are in the presence of God all the time. For this reason the faithful should exercise humility all the time. The faithful should be in a state of adoration of the Father in Spirit as he really is all the time.

Blessing

Blessing is a sacramental of the Church. Blessing is an expression of Christian prayer moving from the Father through Christ to the whole human race from the beginning of the creation. Our Father blesses us by giving us the gifts of life, happiness, fertility, holiness and success in whatever we do. The bishops, priests and deacons of the Church of Christ exercise this sacred action of blessing as the representatives of the Father through Christ.

We in response express our blessing and thanksgiving to God. Our expression of blessing to God is our acknowledgement of his holy name and thanksgiving for his gifts to us through Christ. We further pray for continuing gifts and support of God through Christ. We must be in a state of blessing God and thanksgiving to God all the time as we are receiving the blessing and gifts of God all the time through Christ.

Meditation

In meditation, the mind quietly investigates and asks questions about the Christian life in order to understand it and do what the Lord is asking one to do. The meditation way of prayer requires attentiveness and listening to the Word of God revealed through the Holy Scriptures and saying yes to God and rejecting the Evil One through Christ in the unity of the Holy Spirit.

Meditation engages the whole being: the five senses, thought, mind, body and soul. In meditation, we pass from the movement of thought and the senses to reality; from movement to silence and stillness; from darkness to Light and from egotism to humility and become humble and faithful to God through Christ. The Word of God in this prayer book will help you to meditate on what you read and make it your own by confronting it with yourself through Christ.

Contemplation

In contemplation, the soul mentally and in solitude investigates and asks further questions for deeper experience about the Christian faith, love of God and one another, forgiveness of sins, salvation through our risen Lord and everlasting life. At that stage the Holy Spirit will help you to leave all behind, all senses, feelings, thoughts, reasons and desires and become completely free and detached from all these things and hindrances in order to enter the Kingdom of God through only Christ.

In contemplation, the soul seeks transformation in the image and likeness of God and hope for everlasting life through union with Christ

Jesus and the grace of the Holy Spirit. In that union with Christ in you, God will reveal himself, his glory and heritage to you through Christ. The Word of God in this prayer book will help you to contemplate on what you read and you will become a new person in union with the Christ in you.

Vocal Prayer

In vocal prayer, the soul by the voice and other instruments, often in a group in a public place of worship, seeks unity of the body, soul and spirit in union with Christ.

The soul seeks that unity through vocal prayer by proclaiming the mighty deeds of the Almighty God and the salvation of the whole human race from the Evil One through the grace of the risen Lord. The Word of God in this prayer book will help you to do your vocal prayer through Christ.

How do we know whether what we are doing is prayer to God?

How do we know whether what we are doing is prayer to God? We know by hope and patience through the Holy Spirit. "For it was by hope that we were saved; but if we see what we hope for, then it is not really hope. For which of us hope for something we see? But if we hope for what we do not see, we wait for it with patience. In the same way the Spirit also comes to help us, weak as we are. For we do not know how we ought to pray; the Spirit himself pleads with God for us in groans that words cannot express. And God, who sees into our hearts, knows what the thought of the Spirit is; because the Spirit pleads with God on behalf of his people and in accordance with his will." *Rom 8: 24-27.*

The Christian Liturgy

The liturgy is the work of worshipping the living God in Spirit as he truly is by the people of God through Christ. Through the liturgy, the mysteries of the will and plan of the Father is done by the Father offering his beloved only Son and his Holy Spirit for the salvation of the whole human race from the Evil One for the glory of his holy name. The word "liturgy" means true participation of the assembly of the people of God in the work of worshipping the almighty God in Spirit as he truly is.

In the liturgy, public divine worship of the Father is performed by the Mystical Body of the risen Lord Jesus Christ, the Head of the Church, and its members through the priests and the bishops. Thus, the liturgy is a sacred action by the holy catholic and apostolic Church and the communion of saints for the grace and mercy of God for the whole human race through Christ and through the bishops, priests and pastors of Christ.

The Church of Christ was made known to the whole human race on the day of Pentecost when the Holy Spirit proceeded from the Father and the Son and poured his grace and fruits on the Church and the faithful of the Church. Through the risen Lord, the Father poured into the hearts of the faithful the Gift that embraces all gifts, the Holy Spirit itself.

Every true Christian Church must have its source and goal in the Father through Christ. The whole human race is called for salvation through Christ. If it were not so the risen Lord Jesus Christ, Light from Light and God from God would have said it.

Through the liturgy, all Christian celebrations, the mysteries of the seven Sacramental actions of the Church, prayers, active charity, the declaration of the Christian faith in one invisible and living God, proclamation of the Good News of the Gospel and expressing life in the Spirit of the risen Lord Jesus Christ and his new Law for the people of God, find their source and goal in the Father in union with Christ. Amen.

The Holy Sacrifice of the Mass is that aspect of the liturgy, which has an introductory rite, penitential rite, the liturgy of the Word, the liturgy of the Eucharist, the Communion rite, the rite of peace and a concluding rite. The liturgy of the Eucharist is the central sacrament of the Church.

The word "Mass" is derived from the Latin words *missa est – to be sent away, or to be dismissed,* which are said by the priest at the end of the Latin Mass as a final blessing to dismiss or send away the assembly of the people of God. The expression used by the priest at the end of the English Mass for the Latin *Ite, missa est* takes one of the following forms. "The Mass is ended go in peace." "Go in peace to love and serve the Lord."

The Mass is celebrated by the priests of the Church every day of the week and in particular every Sunday, the Lord's Day, in all the Churches throughout the world where there is an access to a priest in union with Christ. The risen Lord is present in the earthly liturgy as in the liturgy in heaven. In the liturgy in heaven, the celebration is wholly communion and feasting without the signs and the rituals in the earthly liturgy.

The celebration of the liturgy involves sacred signs and symbols, namely, water, fire, candles, washing, anointing with oil, breaking bread, eating the body of Christ through the Holy Communion and drinking the blood of Christ through drinking the wine by the faithful. Song, music and musical instruments are used to glorify the Lord.

The Church recognises different liturgical traditions or rites, namely, the Latin rite (the Roman rite, Ambrosian rite and the rites of certain religious orders), the Alexandrian or Coptic rite, Byzantine rite, Syriac rite, Armenian rite, Maronite rite and the Childean rite. Thus, the Church is flexible as to its rites in the diocese and regions of the world.

The liturgy therefore corresponds to the genius and culture of the people of God anywhere. The mystery celebrated in the liturgy is one and the same on earth as in the heavenly liturgy. But the ritual forms of celebrations are different and unique according to the culture of the people.

Christ himself is in charge of the heavenly liturgy, where everything is perfect; there is no celebration of the seven sacraments as on earth but only eternal feasting in the wedding banquet of the Lamb of God, who takes away all our sin. Amen.

Through the liturgy, the secret and the plan of God is revealed and fulfilled to the glory of God. The liturgy is a memorial of the mystery of salvation through Christ. The liturgy is a response of the Church to the Father for salvation and a means of expressing adoration, praise and thanksgiving to the Father through Christ for our salvation.

The mysterious transforming power of the Holy Spirit is a secret of God in the liturgy and all sacramental actions of the Church. The Holy Spirit like fire transforms into itself everything it touches. The Holy Spirit gives life and fulfilment of prayers and promises to those who accept him in truth as he really is. This work of transformation through sanctification by the Holy Spirit is a mystery and secret of the living God in union with Christ. The secret can only be revealed to you through life in the Spirit in union with Christ.

Where should the liturgy be celebrated?

Where should the earthly liturgy be celebrated? The liturgy is not restricted to any one place; it can be celebrated in any part of the sacred earth on which we live and move and in a church house of prayer, where the faithful can assemble and celebrate the Sacraments in the presence of God. Such a church house should contain (1) the altar, (2) the Eucharist tarbernacle, the Blessed Sacrament of the altar, (3) the sacred chrism (myron) for annointings as a sacramental sign of the seal for the grace of the Holy Spirit. This should be kept in the sanctuary, (4) the oil of annointing the sick be kept in the sanctuary, (5) the chair or Cathedra of the bishop or the priest. (6) the lectern, the space for celebrating the liturgy of the Word of God. (7) the holy water font for reminding the faithful of their Baptismal promises to reject the Evil One. (8) a space for celebration of Baptism (Baptistry). (9) a space for making confession, reconciliation, expressing repentance and receiving forgiveness of sins. (10) a space for the choir and singers. (11) a space for vocal prayer, silent personal meditation and contemplation. (12) a space for all people of God when God "will wipe every tear from their eyes." (13) a space for receiving the Holy Communion. (14) an annexed parish pastoral centre for education and training of the people of God in the parish and for promoting charitable activities in union with Christ. (15) an annexed house for the parish priests. (16) an annexed house for the holy sisters of the Church.

The Lord's Prayer

Our Father, who art in heaven,
Hallowed be thy name;
Thy kingdom come,
Thy will be done on earth as it is in heaven.
Give us this day our daily bread;
And forgive us our trespasses
As we forgive those who trespass against us;
And lead us not into temptation,
But deliver us from evil. Amen.

The Lord is my Shepherd

The Lord is my shepherd;
I have everything I need.
He lets me rest in fields of green grass
and leads me to quiet pools of fresh water.
He gives me new strength.
He guides me in the right paths,

as he has promised.
Even if I go through the deepest darkness,
I will not be afraid, LORD,
for you are with me.
Your shepherd's rod and staff protect me.
You prepare a banquet for me,
where all my enemies can see me;
you welcome me as an honoured guest
and fill my cup to the brim.
I know that your goodness and love
will be with me all my life;
and your house will be my home
as long as I live. (Psalms 23.)

The Hail Mary

Hail Mary, full of grace, the Lord is with thee.
Blessed art thou among women,
and blessed is the fruit of thy womb, Jesus.
Holy Mary, Mother of God,
pray for us sinners,
now and at the hour of our death.

Hail, Holy Queen

Hail, holy Queen, Mother of mercy.
Hail, our life, our sweetness, and our hope.
To you do we cry, poor banished children of Eve.
To you do we send up our sighs,
Mourning and weeping in this valley of tears.
Turn then, most gracious advocate,
Your eyes of mercy towards us,
And after this our exile,
Show unto us the blessed fruit of your womb, Jesus.
O clement, O loving, O sweet virgin Mary.

The Prayer of St. Francis of Assisi

Lord, make me an instrument of your peace:
where there is hatred, let me sow love;
where there is injury, let me sow pardon;
where there is doubt, let me sow faith;
where there is despair, let me give hope;
where there is darkness, let me give light;

where there is sadness, let me give joy.
O Divine Master, grant that I may try
not to be comforted, but to comfort;
not to be understood, but to understand;
not to be loved, but to love.
Because it is in giving that we receive,
it is in forgiving that we are forgiven,
and it is in dying that we are born to eternal life.

The Glory Be

Glory be to the Father,
and to the Son,
and to the Holy Spirit.
As it was in the beginning,
is now, and ever shall be,
world without end. Amen.

Prayer for the Dead

Eternal rest give unto them, O Lord,
and let perpetual light shine upon them.
May they rest in peace. Amen.

An Act of Love of God and Neighbour

O my God, I love you above all things,
with my whole heart and soul,
because you are all good and worthy of all love.
I love my neighbour as myself for the love of you.
I forgive all who have injured me,
and I ask pardon of all whom I have injured.

Prayer is answered in a state of humility and freedom from the world

"Where do all the fights and quarrels among you come from? They come from your desires for pleasure, which are constantly fighting within you. You want things, but you cannot have them, so you are ready to kill; you strongly desire things, but you cannot get them, so you quarrel and fight.

You do not have what you want because you do not ask God for it. And when you ask, you do not receive it, because your motives are bad; you ask for things to use for your own pleasures.

Unfaithful people! Don't you know that to be the world's friend means to be God's enemy? People who want to be the world's friends make themselves God's enemies. Don't think that there is no truth in the scripture that says, "The spirit that God placed in us is filled with fierce desires". But the grace that God gives is even stronger. As the scripture says, "God resists the proud, but gives grace to the humble."

So then, submit to God. Resist the Devil and he will run away from you. Come near to God, and he will come near to you. Wash your hands, you sinners! Purify your hearts, you hypocrites! Be sorrowful, cry, and weep; change your laughter into crying, your joy into gloom ! Humble yourselves before the Lord, and he will lift you up."

Warning against Judging another person and a Fellow-Christian

"Do not criticize one another, my brothers and sisters. If you criticize fellow-Christians or judge them, you criticize the Law and judge it. If you judge the Law, then you are no longer one who obeys the Law, but one who judges it. God is the only lawgiver and judge. He alone can save and destroy. Who do you think you are, to judge someone else?"

Warning for the Rich and the Over-confident person

"Now listen to me, you that say, "Today or tomorrow we will travel to a certain city, where we will stay a year and go into business and make a lot of money." You don't even know what your life tomorrow will be! You are like a puff of smoke, which appears for a moment and then disappears. What you should say is this: "If the Lord is willing we will live and do this or that." But now you are proud, and you boast; all such boasting is wrong.

So then, those who do not do the good they know they should do are guilty of sin." *Jas: 4*

The Parable of the Widow and the Judge

"Then Jesus told his disciples a parable to teach them that they should always pray and never become discouraged.

In a certain town there was a judge who neither feared God nor respected people. And there was a widow in that same town, who kept coming to him and pleading for her rights, saying, "Help me against my opponents!" For a long time the judge refused to act, at last he said to himself, "Even though I don't fear God or respect people, yet because of all the trouble this widow is giving me, I will see to it that she gets her rights. If I don't, she will keep on coming and finally wear me out!"

And the Lord continued, "Listen to what that corrupt judge said. Now, will God not judge in favour of his own people who cry to him day and night for help? Will he be slow to help them? I tell you, he will judge in their favour and do it quickly.

But will the Son of Man find faith on earth when he comes? *Lk 18: 1-8*

CHAPTER ELEVEN

Sacrament of Baptism

"No one can enter the Kingdom of God without being born of water and the Spirit" Jn 3:5

Scriptural source of Baptism in the Holy Spirit of Jesus Christ What is Baptism? Christian initiation. Basic essential rite of Baptism. Essential Elements and Formalities of Baptism. Who can Baptise? Who can receive Baptism? Necessity of Baptism for salvation through Christ. Fruits and grace of Baptism.

Scriptural source of Baptism in the Holy Spirit of Jesus Christ

After the resurrection of Christ, he gave the authority to the Apostles to baptise when he said: "I have been given all authority in heaven and on earth. Go, then, to all peoples everywhere and make them my disciples: baptize them in the name of the Father, the Son, and the Holy Spirit, and teach them to obey everything I have commanded you. And I will be with you always, to the end of the age." *Mat 28: 18-20.*

What is Baptism?

Baptism is a bath that purifies, justifies and sanctifies. Baptism is the first sacramental action of the Church, whereby an individual is born anew and is admitted as a member of the Body of Christ.

Baptism is the gateway to life in the Spirit of Christ. The effect of Baptism is that the faithful is freed from the slavery of sin. The faithful becomes a member of the Christian Community. The faithful is empowered to participate in the salvation mission of Christ and his Church. The faithful is regenerated through the washing by water and renewal by the Holy Spirit. Baptism is the sacrament of faith in the risen Lord Jesus Christ.

Christian Initiation

Baptism, Confirmation and the Eucharist are the three Sacraments of initiation. They lay a sound foundation for the enjoyment of the divine life by the faithful. Baptism makes the faithful a son or daughter of God. The sacrament of Confirmation strengthens the faithful. The sacrament of the Eucharist offers the food of eternal life to the faithful.

Basic Essentials of Baptism in the Latin Rite

In the Latin Church, the essential rite of the sacrament of Baptism is performed by immersion of the candidate in the baptismal water thrice. Alternatively, the water is poured over the candidate's head three times. This triple bath of water is accompanied by the minister's words: "N., I baptize you in the name of the Father, and of the Son, and of the Holy Spirit."

The candidate is anointed with sacred oil of chrism, consecrated by the bishop. This anointing means the gift of the Holy Spirit to the newly baptized candidate.

The white garment worn by the newly baptised candidate means that the candidate has put on Christ and has risen with Christ and brings about the death of the "old man, Adam."

The candle lit from the Easter candle means that Christ has enlightened the newly baptised person and the candidate has become the light of the world on a hill-top, who will enable all in the darkness to see the truth of God and he cannot be hidden.

The newly baptised is entitled to say our Lord's Prayer "Our Father which art in heaven hallowed be their name."

The newly baptised is competent to receive the Holy Communion. He or she is now wearing the wedding garment and can be admitted to the wedding supper and banquet of the Lamb of God who took away our sin. The newly baptised can now eat the food of the new life, the body of Christ and drink the blood of Christ.

The solemn blessing ends the celebration of the Holy Baptism. There would be no Baptism if the essential rites are missing from the celebration.

The Baptismal Promises

Do you reject sin, so as to live in the freedom of God's children? Satan?

I do.

Do you reject the glamour of evil, and refuse to be mastered by sin?

I do.

Do you reject Satan, father of sin and prince of darkness?

I do.

Do you believe in God, the Father almighty, creator of heaven and earth?

I do.

Do you believe in Jesus Christ, his only Son, our Lord, who was born of the Virgin Mary, was crucified, died, and was buried, rose from the dead, and is now seated at the right hand of the Father:

I do.

Do you believe in the Holy Spirit, the holy Catholic Church, the communion of saints, the forgiveness of sins, the resurrection of the body, and life everlasting?

I do.

Essential Elements and Formalities of Baptism

The sign of the cross marks the candidate with the imprint of Christ and means our salvation by Christ by his cross.

The proclamation of the Word of God enlightens the recipient and the congregation with the truth.

The Baptismal Promises. One or more exorcisms are pronounced over the candidate, which means his or her liberation from the Evil One. The candidate is anointed with the oil of catechumens or the minister lays his hand on the candidate. The candidate expressly declared his or her rejection of the Evil One, Satan and all his tricks and empty promises. He or she declared his or her belief in the Holy Trinity and the holy Catholic Church.

The baptismal water is consecrated by a prayer of epiclesis for the occasion or at the Easter Vigil.

Who can Baptize?

The bishop, the priest and deacons can baptise in the Latin Churches. In the case of necessity, any person, including any person who is not baptised, with intention to give baptism for salvation through Christ, can baptise any person in the danger of death.

Who can receive Baptism?

Every person who has not been baptized can be baptized. That means no one can be baptized twice.

Infants can be baptized if their parents are prepared for the occasion. Godparents are optional in infant baptism.

Adults who were prepared through study and participation in the catechism may be baptised.

Necessity of Baptism for salvation through Christ.

Baptism is necessary for salvation through Christ. Those who are not baptised will be saved through the mercy of the God of love, if they seek the truth and do the will of God.

Fruits and grace of Baptism

The fruits and grace of baptism are the purification from sin and freedom from the Evil One. Rebirth and forgiveness of all sins, original sin and all personal sin and all punishment for sin.

CHAPTER TWELVE

Sacrament of Confirmation, Chrismation

"Courage!" he said. "It is I. Don't be afraid" Mark 6: 50

Scriptural source of Confirmation for more activity of the Holy Spirit in the faithful Christian. What is Confirmation? Essential Elements and Formalities of Confirmation. Basic essential rites of Confirmation. Who can give Confirmation? Who can receive Confirmation? Necessity of Confirmation. Fruits and grace of Confirmation.

Scriptural source of Confirmation for more activity of the Holy Spirit in the faithful Christian

The sacrament of Confirmation is for self-renewal and reconstruction. And Jesus said to the apostles, "But when the Holy Spirit comes upon you, you will be filled with power, and you will be witnesses for me in Jerusalem, in all Judea and Samaria, and to the end of the earth." After saying this, he was taken up to heaven as they watched him, and a cloud hid him from their sight.

When the day of Pentecost came, all the believers were gathered together in one place. Suddenly there was a noise from the sky, which sounded like a strong wind blowing, and it filled the whole house where they were sitting. Then they saw what looked like tongues of fire, which spread out and touched each person there. They were all filled with the Holy Spirit and began to talk in other languages, as the Spirit enabled them to speak.

There were Jews living in Jerusalem, religious people who had come from every country in the world. When they heard this noise, a large crowd gathered. They were all excited, because each one of them heard the believers speaking in his or her own language. In amazement and wonder they exclaimed, "These people who are talking like this are Galileans! How is it, then, that all of us hear them speaking in our own native languages? We are from Parthia, Media, and Elam; from Mesopotamia, Judea, and Cappadocia; from Pontus and Asia, from

Phrygia and Pamphylia, from Egypt and the regions of Libya near Cyrene. Some of us are from Rome, both Jews and Gentiles converted to Judaism, and some of us are from Crete and Arabia — yet all of us hear them speaking in our own languages about the great things that God has done!" Amazed and confused, they kept asking each other, "What does this mean?"

But others made fun of the believers, saying, "These people are drunk!"

Peter said to them, "Each one of you must turn away from your sins and be baptized in the name of Jesus Christ, so that your sins will be forgiven; and you will receive God 's gift, the Holy Spirit. For God 's promise was made to you and your children, and to all who are far away — all whom the Lord our God calls to himself." (Acts 1: 8-9; 2: 1-13, 38-39)

What is Confirmation?

Confirmation is the sacramental action of the Church, which completes the act of Christian initiation. Confirmation strengthens the candidate and it perpetuates the grace of Pentecost in the Church. Anointing the candidate with the sacred chrism or myron means the candidate is consecrated and sealed with the Spiritual seal of the Holy Spirit.

The oil means a sign of abundance and joy. That means there is abundance for every one and there is no need to worry about possessions of this world. Oil cleanses and is a sign of healing and health. The seal of the Holy Spirit means the candidate is consecrated with the authority and power of the Holy Spirit. The seal of the holy Spirit marks the Christian with total commitment to Christian life.

Essential Elements and Formalities of Confirmation

The consecration of the sacred chrism is an important formality. It precedes the celebration of the Confirmation but part of it. This consecration is done by the bishop in the course of the Chrism Mass of Holy Thursday for the use of the whole diocese.

The Confirmation begins with the renewal of the baptismal promises and the profession of the Christian faith

In the Roman rite the bishop extends his hands over the whole group of the candidates. This sign means the outpouring of the gift of the Holy Spirit on the candidates. The bishop invokes the outpouring of the Holy Spirit in the following words:

"All-powerful God, Father of our Lord Jesus Christ,
by water and the Holy Spirit
you freed your sons and daughters from sin
and gave them new life.
Send your Holy Spirit upon them
To be their helper and guide.
Give them the spirit of wisdom and understanding,
the spirit of right judgement and courage,
the spirit of knowledge and reverence.
Fill them with the spirit of wonder and awe in your presence.
We ask this through Christ our Lord."

Confirmation is different from Baptism. Baptism means washing away all sins, interior conversion and rebirth. Confirmation is empowerment of the recipient through the Holy Spirit to act as the ambassador of Christ through out the world in the manner and Spirit of Christ for the full life and development of the children of God. Confirmation means total commitment to Christian life.

Basic Essential Rites of Confirmation

The basic essential rites in the Latin rites are anointing of the candidate with Chrism on the forehead, which is done by laying on of the hand, and through the words: "Be sealed with the Gift of the Holy Spirit."

The sign of peace concludes the celebration. This means communion with the bishop and with all the faithful Christians.

Who can give Confirmation?

Originally, the sacramental action of confirmation was reserved to the bishop in the Latin Church. By delegation priests also can give confirmation. If a Christian is in the danger of death, any competent priest may give confirmation.

Who can receive Confirmation?

Every person who was baptised and not yet confirmed can receive Confirmation.Children who have not yet attained the age of discretion or reason, but in the danger of death can receive the sacrament of confirmation.

This concession to children is defended on the ground that age of the body does not necessarily determine the age of the soul. Further, Christ himself says: "Let the children come to me, and do not stop them, because the Kingdom of God belongs to such as these. I assure you that whoever does not receive the Kingdom of God like a child will never enter it." Then he took the children in his arms, placed his hands on each of them, and blessed them. *Mk 10: 14-16.*

The Church encourages sponsorship for recipients of Confirmation. A mature Christian, who has been fully initiated in Baptism, Confirmation and the Holy Communion, may act as a sponsor.

Necessity of Confirmation

The sacrament of Confirmation completes the initiation into the Christian Church, the Body of Christ. The Christian can now participate in the full life in the Spirit of Christ.

The Baptismal grace is made perfect. The recipient is deeply rooted in the Holy Spirit and indelibly marked with the Seal of the Holy Spirit. The recipient has made stronger his or her union with Christ. The recipient is fully armed through the Holy Spirit with the abilities to bear witness for Christ and to defend the Church of Christ.

Fruits and Grace of Confirmation

The recipient receives the full outpouring of the Holy Spirit as was at Pentecost Sunday and the Seal of the Holy Spirit.

The recipient is given response abilities in any trade, profession, vocation, employment and family in union with Christ. The recipient can use all his endowments through self-knowledge or self-awareness. Use is recognition of one's endowments through faith in Jesus Christ.

CHAPTER THIRTEEN

Sacrament of the Eucharist, Blessed Sacrament, Communion in the context of the Holy Sacrifice of the Mass

"The Father and I are one" Jn 10: 30

Scriptural source of the Eucharist bread and wine as the living body and blood of Christ. What is the Sacrament of the Eucharist? Basic essentials of the Eucharist Celebration in the Roman rite. Essential Elements and Formalities of Celebrating the Eucharist in the context of the Holy Sacrifice of the Mass in the Roman rite. Who can celebrate the Eucharist? Who can receive the Holy Communion? Necessity of celebrating the Eucharist. Fruits and grace of receiving the Holy Communion.

Scriptural source of the Eucharist bread and wine as the living body and blood of Christ

Scriptural source of the Eucharist bread and wine as the living body and blood of Christ

The sacrament of the Eucharist is for self-renewal and reconstruction worldwide. Jesus said to them, "I am telling you the truth: if you do not eat the flesh of the Son of Man and drink his blood, you will not have life in yourselves. Those who eat my flesh and drink my blood have eternal life, and I will raise them to life on the last day. For my flesh is the real food; my blood is the real drink. Those who eat my flesh and drink my blood live in me, and I live in them. The living Father sent me, and because of him I live also. In the same way whoever eats me will live because of me. This, then, is the bread that came down from heaven; it is not like the bread that your ancestors ate. They later died, but those who eat this bread will live for ever." What gives life is God 's Spirit; human power is of no use at all. The words I have spoken to you bring God 's life-giving Spirit, yet some of you do not believe. (Jesus knew from the very beginning who were the ones that would not believe and which one would betray him.) And he added, "This is the very reason I told you that no one can come to me unless the Father makes it possible for him to do so." Because of this, many of Jesus' followers turned back and would not go with him any more. So he asked the twelve disciples, "And you — would you also like to leave?" Simon Peter answered him, "Lord, to whom would we go? You have the words that give eternal life. And now we believe and know that you are the Holy One who has come from God." (Jn 6: 53-58, 63-69)

Whenever you go to the Mass and celebrate the Eucharistic Communion, you also go to Calvary and meet Christ. You experience the great Sacrifice of Christ to the Father at Calvary for forgiveness of sins of the whole human race and for reconstruction worldwide.

What is the Sacrament of the Eucharist?

The Eucharist is the sacramental action of our Lord Jesus Christ's own Sacrifice in thanksgiving to his Father with his body, blood and life. Christ laid down his life for his friends, the whole human race, and took it back on the third day on Easter Sunday in his resurrection to the Father.

Thus, Eucharist means thanksgiving to God for the creation, for our salvation through Christ and for cleansing of the whole Universe through the great Sacrifice of Christ on the cross. The Eucharist is the source and summit of Christian life.

What Christians and the Church celebrate ever since is a public replay of that sacramental action in the Mass in memory and presence of Christ. The presence of Christ is manifested in the food of the living bread and wine, which is consumed at the Mass by the recipients of the Holy Communion.Celebrating the Mass means going to Calvery to meet Jesus Christ, our redeemer, and shake hands with him.

Christians believe the consecrated bread and wine is the actual Body and Blood of Christ, the Blessed Sacrament. The bread and the wine are signs of the presence of Christ with us in the celebration. This is an act of faith.

The sharing and consumption of the Holy Communion at the Mass is the final act of the Eucharist. Our consumption of the consecrated bread and wine is our communication with Christ and he with us, and with one another. Through the consumption our mind and body is filled with the grace of the Holy Spirit. The celebration makes us all One in one Body in union with Christ. This means we died with Christ and resurrected with him and are living in the Spirit and presence of Christ.

Basic Essentials of the Eucharist Celebration in the Latin Rite

At the summit of the Eucharist celebration are the bread and wine, which by the words of Christ and the invocation of the Holy Spirit by the minister, become the Body and Blood of Christ. The consecration and the invocation proceeds as follows:

Let your Spirit come upon these gifts to make them holy, so that they may become for us the body of Christ and blood of our Lord Jesus Christ.

Before he was given up to death, a death he freely accepted, he took bread and gave you thanks. He broke the bread, gave it to his disciples, and said:

> TAKE THIS, ALL OF YOU, AND EAT IT: THIS IS MY BODY WHICH WILL BE GIVEN UP FOR YOU.

When supper was ended, he took the cup. Again he gave you thanks and praise, gave the cup to his disciples, and said:

> TAKE THIS, ALL OF YOU, AND DRINK FROM IT: THIS IS THE CUP OF MY BLOOD, THE BLOOD OF THE NEW AND EVERLASTING COVENANT. IT WILL BE SHED FOR YOU AND FOR ALL SO THAT SINS MAY BE FORGIVEN. DO THIS IN MEMORY OF ME.

In the giving and receiving the Holy Communion, the minister says: THE BODY OF CHRIST. The recipient acknowledges: AMEN.

Essential Elements and Formalities of celebrating the Eucharist in the context of the Holy Sacrifice of the Mass in the Latin Rite

All the seven sacraments instituted by Christ may be celebrated during the Holy Sacrifice of the Mass. The Mass is the public assembly of the faithful, the visible people of the Church of Christ in prayer to God through Christ.

The order of the liturgy of the Eucharist Mass follows in outline.

The Eucharist Assembly
All the faithful come together in one place. The head of the assembly is Christ himself, who presides invisibly over every Eucharist celebration. The bishops and the priests act as representatives and agents of Christ in the celebration of the Eucharist. They speak on behalf of Christ.

The Penitential Rite
My brothers and sisters, to prepare ourselves to celebrate the sacred mysteries, let us call to mind our sins.

I confess to almighty God, and to you, my brothers and sisters, that I have sinned through my own fault in my thoughts and in my words, in what I have done, in what I have failed to do; and I asked blessed Mary, ever virgin, all the angels and saints, and you, my brothers and sisters, to pray for me to the Lord our God.

The Liturgy of the Word
The liturgy of the Word means reading from the Old and the New Testaments. This is followed by the homily of the priest. The homily is an exhortation to accept the Word as the Word of God and to put the Word into practice for self-renewal.

Profession of the Christian Faith
The assembly prays on the Apostle's Creed.

The Liturgy of the Eucharist
This is the stage for the presentation of the offering. This means the bread and the wine are brought to the altar for consecration.

The Eucharist Prayer Two for Thanksgiving and Consecration.
Father, it is our duty and our salvation, always and everywhere to give you thanks through your beloved Son, Jesus Christ. He is the Word through whom you made the Universe, the Saviour you sent to redeem us. By the power of the Holy Spirit he took flesh and was born of the Virgin Mary. For our sake he opened his arms on the cross; he put an end to death and revealed the resurrection. In this he fulfilled your will and won for you a holy people. And so we join the angels and the saints in proclaiming your glory as we say:

HOLY, HOLY, HOLY LORD, GOD OF POWER AND MIGHT, HEAVEN AND EARTH ARE FULL OF YOUR GLORY HOSANNA IN THE HIGHEST. BLESSED IS HE OR SHE

WHO COMES IN THE NAME OF THE LORD. HOSANNA IN THE HIGHEST.

The Consecration of the Bread and Wine
These are the essential rites of the Eucharist declared above.

The Communion Rite: The Lamb Banquet
Let us pray with confidence to the Father in the words our Saviour gave us:

Our Father who art in heaven,
hallowed be thy name.
Thy kingdom come,
Thy will be done on earth, as it is in heaven.
Give us this day our daily bread,
And forgive us our trespasses,
As we forgive those who trespass against us,
And lead us not into temptation,
but deliver us from evil.

Deliver us, Lord, from every evil,
and grant us peace in our day.
In your mercy keep us free from sin
and protect us from all anxiety
as we wait in joyful hope
for the coming of our Saviour, Jesus Christ.

For the kingdom, the power, and the glory
are yours, now and for ever.

Rite of Peace

Lord Jesus Christ, you said to your apostles:
I leave you peace, my peace I give you.
Look not on our sins, but on the faith of your Church,
and grant us the peace and unity of your kingdom
where you live for ever and ever. Amen.

May this mingling of the body and blood of our Lord
Jesus Christ bring eternal life to us who receive it.

Lamb of God, you take away the sins of the world:
have mercy on us.
Lamb of God, you take away the sins of the world:
have mercy on us.
Lamb of God, you take away the sins of the world:
have mercy on us.

This is the Lamb of God
who takes away the sins of the world.
Happy are those who are called to his supper.

LORD, I AM NOT WORTHY TO RECEIVE YOU,
BUT ONLY SAY THE WORD AND I SHALL BE HEALED.

Concluding Rite

The Lord be with you.
And also with you.

May almighty God bless you,
The Father, and the Son, and the Holy Spirit.
Amen.

The Mass is ended, go in peace and serve the Lord.

Thanks be to God.

Who can celebrate the Eucharist?

The ministers of the Church may celebrate the Eucharist.
Appointed lay ministers may give the Communion including women.

Who can receive the Holy Communion?

A baptised Catholic Christian, whose sins are forgiven.

Children should not receive the Holy Communion before they attain the age of reason.

Necessity of celebrating the Eucharist

The Eucharist is a thanksgiving to God through Christ. The Eucharist is thanksgiving to God's action for cleansing the world through Christ. It is the response of the human race for worshipping God in Spirit as he truly is through Christ. The Eucharist is celebrated in memory of the great Sacrifice of Christ on the cross for forgiveness of sins. The Eucharist is celebrated to enable the faithful become united with Christ in one Body and to love one another as Christ loves us.

Fruits and grace of receiving the Holy Communion

The Holy Communion increases our union and communication with Christ. It separates us from sin and the Evil One. It cleanses us from the sins and opinions of the ages.

It enables us to become conscious of self-knowledge or self-awareness and to use all the endowments and talents of Christ in our soul to the glory of God. It unites us with the Church, the Body of Christ.

CHAPTER FOURTEEN

Sacrament of Confession, Penance, Reconciliation for Healing and Health

"If you forgive others the wrongs they have done to you, your Father in heaven will also forgive you. But if you do not forgive others, then your Father will not forgive the wrongs you have done." Mat 6: 14-15

Scriptural Source of Forgiveness of sin for self-renewal. What is sin? What is Confession of sin? Basic essential rites of Confession. Essential Elements and Formalities of Confession. Who can forgive sin? Who can make Confession of sin? Fruits and grace of confession and forgiveness of sin.

Scriptural Source of Forgiveness of sin for self-renewal

"If your brother sins against you, go to him and show him his fault. But do it privately, just between yourselves. If he listens to you, you have won your brother back. But if he will not listen to you, take one or two other persons with you, so that every accusation may be upheld by the testimony of two or more witnesses, as the scripture says. And if he will not listen to them, then tell the whole thing to the church. Finally, if he will not listen to the church, treat him as though he were a pagan or a tax collector." *Mat. 18: 15-17.*

"Jesus said to them again, "Peace be with you. As the Father sent me, so I send you." Then he breathed on them and said, "Receive the Holy Spirit. If you forgive people's sins, they are forgiven; if you do not forgive them, they are not forgiven." *Jn 20:21-23.*

"The Parable of the Unforgiving Servant. Then Peter came to Jesus and asked, "Lord, if my brother keeps on sinning against me, how many times do I have to forgive him? Seven times?"

"No, not seven times," answered Jesus, "but seventy times seven, because the Kingdom of heaven is like this. Once there was a king who decided to check on his servants' accounts. He had just begun to do so when one of them was brought in who owed him millions of pounds. The servant did not have enough to pay his debt, so the king ordered him to be sold as a slave, with his wife and his children and all that he had, in order to pay the debt. The servant fell on his knees before the king. "Be patient with me," he begged, "and I will pay you everything!" The king felt sorry for him, so he forgave him the debt and let him go.

Then the man went out and met one of his fellow-servants who owed him a few pounds. He grabbed him and started choking him. "Pay back what you owe me!" he said. His fellow-servant fell down and begged him, "Be patient with me, and I will pay you back!" But he refused; instead, he had him thrown into jail until he should pay the debt. When the other servants saw what had happened, they were very upset and went to the king and told him everything. So he called the servant in. "You worthless slave!" he said. "I forgave you the whole amount you owed me, just because you asked me to. You should have had mercy on your fellow-servant, just as I had mercy on you." The king was very angry, and he sent the servant to jail to be punished until he should pay back the whole amount."

And Jesus concluded, "That is how my Father in heaven will treat every one of you unless you forgive your brother from your heart." *Matt 18: 21-35.*

What is sin?

Sin is any wilful action, word, thought, or omission forbidden by the law of God. Sin is rejection of God by a created being and opposition of God. Sin is an abuse of the freedom that God gives to created beings so that they may choose to love God and one another and not the Evil One. Sin prevents contact of God by the sinner.

The Ten Commandments and the Lord's Sermon on the Mount contain the laws of God. Breach of these laws and prohibitions constitutes sin.

Sin wounds the sinner, the person who is the victim of the sinner and the whole Church. So sin is against the sinner, his or her neighbour and the Church, the Body of Christ.

The Catholic Church is the Pope, the bishops and all ministers of the Church and deacons in Holy Orders and all the faithful. The Pope is the head of the Catholic Church and the Vicar of Christ.

There are three kinds of sin: original sin, mortal sin and venial sin. Original sin is that sin we inherited from Adam and Eve. Mortal sin and venial sin are sins we have personally committed. Mortal sin is a serious sin, which one has wilfully committed and which one has freely chosen to commit. This is intentional sin. If not repented the sinner may go to hell.

Venial sin is a serious sin, which one commits without considering the consequences of what one is doing. The sinner has no *mens rea* or guilty mind. This is unintentional sin. Mortal sin and venial sin are also described as actual sin in contrast with original sin we inherited from Adam and Eve.

Sin or evil arises from the imperfect nature of the human being. Hence the need for self-knowledge and our response abilities for good and against evil. Constant daily self-renewal can overcome sin and evil.

What is Confession of Sin?

Confession means disclosure of sin by the sinner to a minister of the Church in the Confession process of the Church and receiving forgiveness through absolution.

All sins committed before baptism are forgiven at baptism. Sin committed after baptism must be confessed.

The Sacrament of Reconciliation is God's grace of mercy, forgiveness and healing of the wound the sinner has inflicted. The term Reconciliation replaced Penance and Confession since the second Vatican Council. Reconciliation is an apt description because it conveys the sense of restoration of good relations between the sinner and God after disclosure and forgiveness of one's sin.

Basic Essential rites of Confession

Four steps lead to confession of sin: act of sorrow, confession of sin to a priest, forgiveness through absolution and satisfaction or penance.

Act of sorrow is an expression of sorrow of the penitent for the sin committed and a resolution not to commit further sin.

Confession of sin to a priest is the disclosure or admission of sin to a priest. The admission frees one from being a captive of sin and facilitates reconciliation with God, neighbour and the Church.

Absolution of the priest takes away sin and frees the sinner from the Evil One. The absolution formula is as follows:

> God, the Father of mercies,
> through the death and the resurrection of his Son
> has reconciled the world to himself
> and sent the Holy Spirit among us

for the forgiveness of sins;
through the ministry of the Church
may God give you pardon and peace,
and I absolve you from your sins
in the name of the Father, and of the Son, and of the Holy Spirit.

Satisfaction or penance which may be imposed by the priest may include restoration of stolen goods, restoration of reputation of some one slandered or defamed, payment of compensation for injuries or wound inflicted by the sinner.

Further, satisfaction may include prayer, making an offering, doing works of mercy, providing service to neighbour and voluntary self-denial.

Essential Elements and Formalities of Confession

The sacrament of Confession is a liturgical action like all the sacraments of the Church. The elements and formalities include: a greeting and blessing from the priest or the confessor, reading the Word of God and the delivery of the homily, the imposition and acceptance of penance, the absolution of the priest, a prayer of thanksgiving and praise of God for his mercy and love and dismissal of the penitent with the blessing of the priest.

Who can forgive sin?

Priests and bishops who have received the faculty of absolving from the authority of the Church can forgive sin in the name of Jesus Christ. In danger of death of a penitent, priests not approved by the Church to hear confession may forgive sin in the name of Christ.

Who can make confession of sin?

Any baptized Christian who has attained the age of discretion and understands the consequences of right and wrong and the prohibitions of the Church in the Ten Commandments and the Lord's Sermon on the Mount can make confession of sin.

Fruits and grace of confession and forgiveness of sin

Penitent obtains reconciliation with God, Christ, the Church and recovery of lost grace.

Penitent gets remission of the eternal punishment incurred by mortal sins. Penitent receives peace, serenity of conscience, spiritual consolation and an increase of spiritual strength and energy for the Christian battle for self-renewal against the Evil One.

Penitent receives self-renewal in any trade, profession, vocation, employment and family and will be able to respond freely to his or her goals and actualise them in union with Christ.

CHAPTER FIFTEEN

Sacrament of Anointing the Sick for Healing and Health

"Your Father in heaven knows that you need all these things. Instead, be concerned above everything else with the Kingdom of God and with what he requires of you, and he will provide you with all these other things" Matt 6: 32-33

Scriptural Source of the Sacrament of Anointing the Sick. What is the Sacrament of Anointing the Sick? Basic essential rite of Anointing the Sick. Essential Elements and Formalities of Anointing the Sick. Who can administer the Sacrament of Anointing the Sick? Who can receive the Sacrament of Anointing the Sick? Fruits and grace of receiving the sacrament of Anointing the Sick.

Scriptural Source of the Sacrament of Anointing the Sick

"Are any of you ill? You should send for the Church elders, who will pray for them and rub olive oil on them in the name of the Lord. This prayer made in faith will heal the sick; the Lord will restore them to health, and the sins they have committed will be forgiven. So then, confess your sins to one another and pray for one another, so that you will be healed. The prayer of a good person has a powerful effect." *Jas. 5:14-16.*

"So they went out and preached that people should turn away from their sins. They drove out many demons, and rubbed olive oil on many sick people and healed them." *Mk 6: 12-13.*

"Believers will be given the power to perform miracles: they will drive out demons in my name; they will speak in strange tongues; if they pick up snakes or drink any poison, they will not be harmed; they will place their hands on sick people, who will get well." *Mk 16: 17-18.*

"Heal the sick, bring the dead back to life, heal those who suffer from dreaded skin diseases, and drive out demons. You have received without paying, so give without being paid." *Mat 10: 8.*

What is the Sacrament of Anointing the Sick?

This is the Sacramental action of healing of the Church. By the sacred anointing of the sick and prayer of the priests, the Church commits those who are sick to our risen Lord Jesus Christ, the physician of all seasons, to raise them up and to heal them.

The sacrament gives a special grace of God to the Christian experiencing the difficulties inherent in serious illness or old age.

Basic Essential rite of Anointing the Sick in the Roman rite.

The sacrament is given to the faithful who are seriously ill by anointing them on the forehead and hands with duly blessed olive oil or oil from other plants by the bishop, or his delegate or any priest in emergency. The minister should say only once the following:

"Through this holy anointing may the Lord in his love and mercy help you with the grace of the Holy Spirit. May the Lord who frees you from sin save you and raise you up."

Essential Elements and Formalities of Anointing the Sick

This sacrament like all the sacraments is a liturgical action of the Church, irrespective of whether it takes place in hospital, in the family home or church, for a whole group of sick persons or for a single sick person.

It is often celebrated within the Eucharist and if possible it is preceded with the sacrament of Penance.

Who can administer the Sacrament of Anointing the Sick?

Priests of the Church who are authorised by the bishop are entitled to anoint the Sick. In silence they lay hands on the Sick; they pray over them in the faith of the Church.

Who can receive the Sacrament of Anointing the Sick?

The sacrament is available to those Christians who are seriously ill but does not mean that they should be at the point of death.

If the sick Christian who received the sacrament recovers his or her health, he or she can in the case of subsequent serious illness receive the sacrament again and the sacrament may be repeated if the condition of the faithful becomes more serious.

It is appropriate to receive the sacrament prior to a serious surgical operation. The elderly whose infirmity becomes more pronounced may receive the sacrament and could repeat as necessary.

In addition to this sacrament the Church gives the faithful who are about to depart from this life the Eucharist as viaticum because our Lord said: "Those who eat my flesh and drink my blood have eternal life, and I will raise them to life on the last day. For my flesh is the real food; my blood is the real drink. Those who eat my flesh and drink my blood live in me, and I live in them. The living Father sent me, and because of him I live also. In the same way whoever eats me will live because of me." Jn 6:54-57.

Fruits and grace of receiving the sacrament of Anointing the Sick

The sacrament of Anointing the Sick offers a special grace of God with the following consequences:

The uniting of the sick faithful to the Passion of Christ, for his own good and the good of the whole Church.

The strengthening, peace and courage to endure in a Christian manner the suffering of illness or old age.

The forgiveness of sins, if the faithful was not able to obtain it through the sacrament of Reconciliation.

The restoration of health, if it is conducive to the salvation of the soul of the faithful.

The preparation for passing over to the Father in eternal life.

CHAPTER SIXTEEN

Sacrament of Marriage and the Family under the Grace of God

"My commandment is this: love one another, just as I love you. The greatest love a person can have for his friends is to give his life for them." Jn 15: 12-13

1. Marriage or Matrimony as a Christian Sacrament and Sciptual source. 2. Special Agreement between a man and a woman. 3. With Full Essential rite of Marriage and Matrimonial Consent. 4. The Love of the Spouses requires Unity and Indissolubility of the Marriage. 5. The Love of the Spouses requires Faithfulness of the spouses to their Marriage Promise of Total Commitment. 6. The Love of the Spouses requires Openness to Fertility, Procreation and Education of Offspring in a Christian Family. 7. Essential Formalities of Sacrament of Marriage. 8. Who can confer Sacrament of Marriage? 9. Who can be a party to the Sacrament of Marriage? 10. Necessity of Sacrament of Marriage. 11. Fruits and grace of Sacrament of Marriage. 12. Sexual activity outside Marriage is a Sin against God and one 's Neighbour 13. Marriage and the Family under the Regime of sin and the Grace of God through Christ.

1. Marriage or Matrimony as a Christian Sacrament and Scriptual source.

Marriage or Matrimony is a Christian Sacrament implied in a special agreement whereby a man and a woman freely choose with their full matrimonial consent to establish a partnership between themselves for the benefit of the spouses and for procreation and education of offspring in a Christian family.

The Vocation of Marriage

The vocation of marriage is inherent in the nature of man and woman from the beginning of the creation by God. God created man and woman out of love and called them to love each other as God loves them. Thus, marriage is a sacred institution and sacrament of God; it is not a human institution.

Couples freely choose to adopt the sacrament by special agreement between the parties. The marriage and the family regime can experience disorder of evil around and within. This disorder can be overcome by the grace of God through faith in God and in Jesus Christ.

Marriage is a Christian Sacrament

What is a sacrament? A sacrament is a visible sign or institution established by God through Christ to give grace. Thus, the seven sacraments established by Christ are the Eucharist, Marriage, Baptism, Confirmation, Confession, Anointing the Sick and Holy Orders.

The human being is created in the image and likeness of God.

God is love. Love is creative.
Nobody has ever seen God.
According to revelation through faith,
human beings are created by God
in the image and likeness of God:

> "So God created human beings,
> making them to be like himself.
> He created them male and female." *Gen. 1:27*

The Original Marriage Union

It is not good that man should be alone; he needs a companion, a partner, a counterpart, his equal, a helpmate:

> "Then the Lord God made the man fall into a deep sleep,
> and while he was sleeping,
> he took out one of the man's ribs and closed up the flesh.
> He formed a woman out of the rib and brought her to him.
> Then the man said:
>
> "At last, here is one of my own kind -
> bone taken from my bone, and
> flesh from my flesh.
> "Woman" is her name because she
> was taken out of man."
>
> That is why a man leaves his father and mother
> and is united with his wife,

and they become one.
The man and the woman were both naked,
but they were not embarrassed." *Gen. 21: 21-25*

The significance of "one of the man's ribs" is that Adam is made to the image of God, and Eve to the image of Adam. "But I want you to understand that Christ is supreme over every man, the husband is supreme over his wife, and God is supreme over Christ." *1 Cor 11: 3.*

Indissolubility of Christian Marriage

Indissolubility of marriage means impossibility of separating the spouses' community of persons in the marriage. So they were no longer two, but one flesh and bone taken from my bone and flesh from my flesh. It is love, which is indivisible and exclusive to the parties for life. This is the evidence of indissolubility of Christian marriage and our Lord Jesus Christ confirmed it when he said:

> "Haven't you read the scripture that says
> that in the beginning the Creator made people male and female?
> And God said, "for this reason a man will leave his father and
> mother and unite with his wife, and the two will become one."
> So they are no longer two, but one.
> No human being must separate, then, what God has joined
> together. *Mat 19: 4-6*

The Power of Love

> "Close your heart to every love but mine;
> hold no one in your arms but me.
> Love is as powerful as death;
> Passion is as strong as death itself.
> It bursts into flame
> And burns like a ranging fire.
> Water cannot put it out;
> No flood can drown it.
> But if anyone tried to buy love with wealth,
> Contempt is all they would get. *Songs of Songs 8: 6-7*

Proactive Responsibilities of the spouses

Marriage is a responsibility. The spouses must have response abilities to each other and the whole world. This means:

"Submit yourselves to one another because of your reverence for

Christ. Wives, submit to your husbands as to the Lord. For a husband has authority over his wife just as Christ has authority over the Church; and Christ is himself the Saviour of the Church, his Body. And so wives must submit completely to their husbands just as the Church submits itself to Christ.

Husbands, love your wives just as Christ loved the Church and gave his life for it. He did this to dedicate the Church to God by his word, after making it clean by washing it in water, in order to present the Church to himself in all its beauty – pure and faultless, without spot or wrinkle or any other imperfection. Men ought to love their wives just as they love their own bodies. A man who loves his wife loves himself. (People never hate their own bodies. Instead, they feed them and take care of them, just as Christ does the Church; for we are members of his Body.)

As the scripture says, "For this reason a man will leave his father and mother and unite with his wife, and the two will become one." There is a deep secret truth revealed in this scripture, which I understand as applying to Christ and the Church. But it also applies to you: every husband must love his wife as himself, and every wife must respect her husband." *Eph 5: 21-33.*

Be Fruitful and Multiply

The marriage must be open to fertility. God blessed man and woman. God bless this love and it is the intention of God
that the couples should be fruitful and he said:

> "Have many children,
> so that your descendants will live all over the earth
> and bring it under their control" *Gen. 1: 28.*

Is Divorce or Remarriage Permissible in a Christian Marriage?

Divorce is not permissible because no human being should separate what God has joined together. "Jesus answered, "Moses gave you permission to divorce your wives because you are so hard to teach. But it was not like that at the time of creation." *Mat 19: 8.*

Thus, it is breach of the Law of God to divorce a spouse. Remarriage is not permissible by the Church because divorce is not possible; one can bite the apple only once. The Church's sanction is to refuse Eucharistic Communion to the parties on remarriage.

Self-knowledge through Love

"I may be able to speak the languages of human beings and even of angels, but if I have no love, my speech is no more than a noisy gong or a clanging bell. I may have the gift of inspired preaching; I may have all knowledge and understand all secrets; I may have all the faith needed to move mountains - but if I have no love, I am nothing. I may give away everything I have, and even give up my body to be burnt - but if I have no love, this does me no good.

Love is patient and kind; it is not jealous or conceited or proud; love is not ill-mannered or selfish or irritable; love does not keep a record of wrongs; love is not happy with evil, but is happy with the truth. Love never gives up; and its faith, hope, and patience never fail.

Love is eternal. There are inspired messages, but they are temporary; there are gifts of speaking in strange tongues, but they will cease; there is knowledge, but it will pass. For our gifts of knowledge and of inspired messages are only partial; but when what is perfect comes, then what is partial will disappear.

When I was a child, my speech, feelings, and thinking were all those of a child; now that I have grown up, I have no more use for childish ways. What we see now is like a dim image in a mirror; then we shall see face to face. What I know now is only partial; then it will be complete - as complete as God's knowledge of me.

Meanwhile these three remain: faith, hope, and love; and the greatest of these is love." *1 Cor 13.*

Love One Another

"Dear friends, let us love one another,
because love comes from God.
Whoever loves is a child of God and knows God.
Whoever does not love does not know God,
for God is love.

And God showed his love for us
by sending his only Son into the world,
so that we might have life through him.
This is what love is: it is not that we have loved God,
but that he loved us and sent his Son
to be the means by which our sins are forgiven.

Dear friends, if this is how God loved us,
then we should love one another.

No one has ever seen God,
but if we love one another,
God lives in union with us,
and his love is made perfect in us.

We are sure that we live in union with God
and that he lives in union with us,
because he has given us his Spirit." *1 Jn 4: 7-13.*

"There is no fear in love;
perfect love drives out all fear.
So then, love has not been made perfect
in anyone who is afraid,
because fear has to do with punishment." *1 Jn 4: 18.*

"If we say we love God,
but hate our brothers and sisters, we are liars.
For people cannot love God,
whom they have not seen,
if they do not love their brothers and sisters,
whom they have seen.
The command that Christ has given us is this:
all who love God must love their brother or sister also."
1 Jn 4: 20-21

2. Special Agreement between a Man and a Woman

The agreement of the spouses to marry one another is special because it is an agreement of public interest; it is governed by the law of God; it is binding for the whole life and it is indissoluble. God himself has determined its beginning and end. It is an agreement which changes the status of the parties from unmarried to married status.

Further, it is special because it is unlike an agreement for sale or purchase of goods and services for a valuable consideration. Money is generally the consideration for the exchange of goods and services.

On the contrary, money is not a consideration for marriage or exchange of love between a man and a woman. Love of the partners for one another should be strong enough to support the Marriage for life. Love is Devine.

The agreement is special because Christ himself elevated it to the status of a sacrament. The agreement and the celebration of the marriage involve the presence of Christ. The presence of our Lord at the wedding at Cana gives the special agreement of marriage a special importance. The agreement gives grace to the parties.

3. With Full Essential Rite of Marriage and Matrimonial Consent

The parties to the marriage must firstly be free to marry and not under any constraint. Secondly both parties must freely determine and express their personal consent to marry.

If any of these two essential elements are wanting the marriage will be declared null and void. Null and void means there was no change of status of the parties because the marriage never existed and the parties are free to marry to another person.

Free to marry and not under any constraint means that there should be no restriction on the parties to marry each other. This restriction may be imposed by the law of the Church or ecclesiastical law or the law of the land. If one of the parties or both were married persons they could not marry again. If the parties are within prohibited degrees of marriage they could not undergo a valid marriage. Thus, one cannot marry his daughter, sister, mother, aunt, uncle, brother, or father. In some cultures one cannot marry one's cousin but this may be permitted in some cultures.

Both parties must freely determine and express their personal consent means both parties must freely exchange consent to marry one another. There is no proxy consent and consent must be personal. This consent is indispensable and if it is absent the marriage is null and void, that means the marriage never existed.

The personal consent involves agreement on personal community of the parties. That means the human act by which the partners mutually give themselves to one another for life. There are various formulas for expressing free consent of the parties. Every culture, region, or country has its own formula. The following two formulas illustrate the point:

I, N., take you, N., to be my husband (wife). I promise to be true to you in good times and in bad, in sickness and in health. I will love you and honour you all the days of my life.

or

Priest: N., do you take N. for your lawful wife (husband), to love and to hold, from this day forward, for better, for worse, for richer, for poorer, in sickness and in health, until death do you part?

Recipient: I do.

The consent must not be given out of any external fear or pressure or undue influence. Lack of true consent makes the marriage invalid.

The priest who assists in the celebration of the marriage receives the consent of the partners on behalf of the Church. The sacrament of marriage is a public matter.

4. The Love of the Spouses requires Unity and Indissolubility of the Marriage

Marriage love means a total commitment of the spouses to each other for the common good of the spouses. Everything each partner has goes into that total commitment without reservation and condition.

The goal of the spouses is to achieve an unbreakable union; a unity which goes beyond union in one flesh and to form one heart and one immortal soul. Marriage love therefore requires unity, faithfulness and openness to fertility and procreation.

The love of the spouses requires unity and indissolubility of the marriage because " they are no longer two, but one." The love of the spouses requires the spouses' community of persons, which embraces their entire life. The marriage is irrevocable so that the spouses can become witnesses of the love of God for the whole human race.

Physical separation of the spouses is permissible by the Church when it becomes impossible for the spouses to live together. In the event of physical separation, the spouses still remain married in the presence of God. The spouses cannot enter into a valid second marriage union.

Can the spouses obtain a civil divorce and celebrate a second civil marriage? This possibility is open to the spouses. The Church does not recognise such a divorce and the second marriage. The Church follows the teachings of Christ when he said:

" A man who divorces his wife and marries another woman commits adultery against his wife. In the same way, a woman who divorces her husband and marries another man commits adultery." *Mk 10: 11-12.*

Our Lord Jesus Christ said: "It was also said, "Anyone who divorces his wife must give her a written notice of divorce." But now I tell you: if a man divorces his wife, for any cause other than her unfaithfulness, then he is guilty of making her commit adultery if she marries again; and the man who marries her commits adultery also." *Matt 5: 31-32.*

The guilty spouses are in sin. Therefore, the guilty spouses cannot receive the Holy Communion. They cannot exercise certain responsibilities in the Church. The Sacrament of Reconciliation and Penance could be granted to the spouses if they repented for violating their marriage union. In that case they must be committed to live in complete restraint of sexual intercourse.

5. The Love of the Spouses requires Faithfulness of the Spouses to their Marriage Promise of Total Commitment.

The love of the spouses requires inviolable fidelity of the spouses. The mutual marriage promise of the spouses imposes this obligation on them. Marriage union means mutual giving of the partners to each other for life.

Life means everlasting life. The spouses are expected to be faithful to one another as Christ is faithful to the Church. Love is irrevocable.

The sixth commandment: thou shall not commit adultery must be religiously observed by the spouses.

6. The Love of the Spouses requires Openness to Fertility, Procreation and Education of offspring in a Christian Family.

Children are the crowning gift of marriage. They contribute to the good of the parents. Thus, God blessed man and woman with the words: "Have many children, so that your descendants will live all over the earth and bring it under their control."

Parents are the first educators of their children. Parents should freely determine their children's education and the quality of education they should give to their children. The objectives of education are stated in Article 26(2) of the Universal Declaration of Human Rights as follows:

"Education shall be directed to the full development of the human personality and to the strengthening of respect for human rights and fundamental freedoms. It shall promote understanding, tolerance and friendship among all nations, racial or religious groups, and shall partner the activities of the United Nations for the maintenance of peace."

The Christian family and home is the first place where children are taught the profession of the Christian faith. Thus, the family home is the domestic church. The Christian family is a community of prayer and the grace of God; it is a school of love of God and neighbour. Regular prayer ensures family unity and guarantees health, peace and prosperity of the family.

7. Essential Formalities of Sacrament of Marriage.

In the Latin rite, the marriage is celebrated during the Holy Sacrifice of the Mass. "It is therefore fitting that the spouses should seal their consent to give themselves to each other through the offering of their own lives by uniting it to the offering of Christ for his Church made present in the Eucharistic sacrifice, and by receiving the Eucharist so that, communicating in the same Body and the same Blood of Christ, they may form but "one body" in Christ." (Catechism of the Catholic Church (Veritas 1994) 1621 page 363)

The bride and the groom are expected to prepare themselves for the celebration of the marriage by the sacrament of Confession and Penance. At the Mass they receive the Holy Communion. The nuptial blessing is a symbol of the seal of the Holy Spirit of the love of the spouses in Christ.

The priest or his delegate acts as the official witness of the Church. It is the duty of the official witness of the Church to receive the public consent of the spouses on behalf of the Church. The best man and the matron of honour receive the public consent of the spouses on behalf of the community at large.

Both spouses do exchange rings to mark their mutual and exclusive love for one another. The ring is a valuable symbol of love for the spouses.

The matrimonial consent of the spouses is the only essential formality, which can render the marriage null and void and invalid, if not observed. Receiving the sacrament of Penance and celebrating the marriage during the Mass and the rest of the formalities are essential formalities, which do not render the marriage invalid if not observed.

8. Who can confer the Sacrament of Marriage?

In the Latin Church, the bride and the bridegroom mutually confer the Sacrament of Marriage on each other by expressing their matrimonial consent before the Church.

Thus, the critical moment of conferring the sacrament on one another is the time the bride and the bridegroom completed saying the " I do ". The marriage union is then sealed by the power of the Holy

Spirit. What God has united nobody can separate.

9. Who can be a party to the sacrament of Marriage?

Difference of confession of faith between the parties does not constitute a barrier to Catholic Christian marriage. Three categories of sacrament of Marriage prevail: 1. Marriage between two faithful baptized Catholic partners. 2. Mixed marriage, that is marriage between a Catholic and a baptized non-Catholic partner. 3. Disparity of cult marriage, that is marriage between a Catholic and a non-baptized partner.

Mixed marriage and disparity of cult marriage have inherent problem of disunity in the family from the start of the marriage. In the case of a mixed marriage, the partners are united in what is common to the partners in faith in the Holy Trinity and divided by what separates them in methodology of worship and Apostolic succession. This is evidence of the need for Christian unity. In the case of disparity of cult marriage, the partners are divided about their faith, about their understanding of the nature of marriage.

Mixed marriage needs express permission of the Church authorities. Disparity of cult marriage needs express dispensation for the validity of the marriage.

In both mixed and disparity of cult marriage, the partners would agree that the Catholic partner should have the obligation for the baptism and education of the children of the marriage in the Catholic Church.

By the grace of God, all the three categories of marriage can happily achieve the goals of a Christian marriage. The three categories depend on the grace of God and not law and nobody knows the terms on which God gives grace to people.

10. Necessity of Sacrament of Marriage.

The sacrament of Marriage is a necessity for those who choose to accept participation in the divine economy of procreation so that the human race can "Be fruitful and multiply."

One is not expected to have children of God without Christian marriage according to the teachings of the Church. The Sacrament of Reconciliation and Penance corrects the error of parents who participate in procreation without Christian marriage. Procreation is not the only goal of indissoluble marriage. Procreation is a gift of God.

Apart from the goal of procreation, sacrament of Marriage is not a necessity. One is free to choose. Our Lord Jesus Christ said: "This teaching does not apply to everyone, but only to those to whom God has given it. For there are different reasons why men cannot marry: some, because they were born that way; others, because men made them that way; and others do not marry for the sake of the Kingdom of heaven. Let him who can accept this teaching do so." *Matt 19: 11-12.*

Saint Paul tackled the question with vigour when he said: "Now, to deal with the matters you wrote about. A man does well not to marry. But because there is so much immorality, every man should have his own wife, and every woman should have her own husband. A man should fulfil his duty as a husband, and a woman should fulfil her duty as a wife, and each should satisfy the other's needs.

A wife is not the master of her own body, but her husband is; in the same way a husband is not the master of his own body, but his wife is. Do not deny yourself to each other, unless you first agree to do so for a while in order to spend your time in prayer; but then resume normal marital relations. In this way you will be kept from giving in to Satan's temptation because of your lack of self-control.

I tell you this not as an order, but simply as a concession. Actually I would prefer that all of you were as I am; but each one has a special gift from God, one person this gift, another one that gift.

Now, to the unmarried and to the widows I say that it would be better for you to continue to live alone as I do. But if you cannot restrain your desires, go ahead and marry – it is better to marry than to burn with passion.

For married people, I have a command, which is not my own but the Lord's: a wife must not leave her husband; but if she does, she must remain single or else be reconciled to her husband; and a husband must not divorce his wife.

To the others I say (I, myself, not the Lord): if a Christian man has a wife who is an unbeliever and she agrees to go on living with him, he must not divorce her. And if a Christian woman is married to a man who is an unbeliever and he agrees to go on living with her, she must not divorce him. For the unbelieving husband is made acceptable to God by being united to his wife, and the unbelieving wife is made acceptable to God by being united to her Christian husband.

If this were not so, their children would be like pagan children; but as it is, they are acceptable to God. However, if the one who is not a believer wishes to leave the Christian partner, let it be so. In such cases the Christian partner, whether husband or wife, is free to act. God has called to you to live in peace.

How can you be sure, Christian wife, that you will not save your husband? Or how can you be sure, Christian husband, that you will not save your wife?" *1 Cor 7: 1-16.*

11. Fruits and Grace of Sacrament of Marriage

The gift of children, divine love between the spouses and a special and general divine grace are the three fruits and grace of the sacrament of Marriage.

Firstly, the consummation of the marriage with gift of a child means the marriage is accepted and blessed by God as it was in the beginning.

Secondly, the matrimonial consent of the couples is sealed by God. From that consent arises an institution of Marriage regulated by divine law. The love between the spouses is unified in the mystery and unity of divine love. Thus, a marriage cannot be dissolved by any human being.

Thirdly, Christ is the source of the special and general grace of the spouses. The special grace makes perfect in the flesh and in the spirit the love between the spouses. The general grace is expressed by the Church in the following terms:

"Christ dwells with them, gives them the strength to take up their crosses and so follow him, to rise again after they have fallen, to forgive one another, to bear one another's burdens, to "be subject to one another out of reverence for Christ" and to love one another with supernatural, tender and fruitful love. In the joys of their love and family life he gives them here on earth a foretaste of the wedding feast of the Lamb" in heaven. (Catechism of the Catholic Church, ibid, 1642 at page 367).

12. Sexual activity outside Marriage is a Sin against God and one 's Neighbour

Sexual activity is permissible only in Marriage for life between two persons of opposite sex. Outside that relationship, any sexual activity is wrong and it is a sin against the Church of Christ, God and your neighbour.

Sexual activity outside Marriage is forbidden by God. Marriage works better if the partners do not have sexual intercourse with each other before Marriage or with another person of the opposite sex before marriage.

Unholy sexual intercourse with another person of the opposite sex before Marriage increases the chance of further unholy intercourse with another person during Marriage. Such promiscuity clouds right judgement of the sinner. "So then, submit to God. Resist the Devil, and he will run away from you." (James 4: 7). Avoid temptation by all means, if you cannot resist it.

Sexual activity outside Marriage runs the risk of abortion. Abortion is killing of unborn child. Abortion is prohibited under the fifth commandment. Thou shall not kill.

Christian hospital workers and others similarly situated are entitled to refuse participation in abortion operations in the hospitals and other premises where abortion is authorised by the law of the land on the ground of conscience and religious belief.

Sexual activity in Marriage is blessed by God when he said, "Be fruitful and multiply." Adam had sexual intercourse with his wife, Eve, and she became pregnant with a child and bore Cain only after the Fall. Later Eve gave birth to another son called Abel. (Gen. 4: 1 -2.)

Sexual activity includes any preparation and invitation for sex, exposure of the body to the opposite sex, discussion of sex with a view to promoting unholy sexual activity outside Marriage and actual sexual intercourse between two persons of the opposite sex. Sex education is not sexual activity.

Sexual activity, like money and power, has become an idol. The media is loaded with uninvited information about sexual activity. That is idolatry. Some women dress to expose their body and soul to public spectacle. That is another idolatry. The family home has become a cockpit in the absence of love. That is idolatry!

Homosexuality is against the sexual plan and order of God; it is a sin against God, the Church and one 's neighbour. Homosexuality is anal intercourse between one man and another man or a sexual perversion between one woman and another woman. Homosexuality must not be practised outside marriage or during marriage.

The Old Testament prohibits homosexuality. The offence carried capital punishment. (Leviticus 18: 22; 20: 13).

Homosexuality is a sin like any other sin. St Paul is not slow to point it out: "Do not fool yourselves; people who are immoral or who worship idols or are adulterers or are homosexual perverts or who steal or are greedy or are drunkards or who slander others or are thieves — none of these will possess God 's Kingdom" (1 Cor 6: 9-10)

Homosexuality generates HIV/AIDS virus, which kills. Homosexuals abuse the freedom of choice God gives the human race. They need salvation and repentance just like any other sinner since Adam and Eve. Homosexuals should be accepted as Christ would accept them. The love of God is stronger than sin. The Church asks those who are of homosexual nature to live a celibate life

Sex outside marriage among teenagers produces unexpected pregnancies and poverty, which must be counteracted. It is desirable to remain a virgin until marriage. Having a baby is important but it could be delayed until marriage. Parents must ensure that their teenagers do not suffer from deprivation. Deprivation leads to high pregnancy rates.

The number of babies born to teenagers in Africa is not known. But the population of Africa is about 750 million people, which is three times higher than the population of Europe or the United States of America.. The number of babies born to teenagers in the United Kingdom is twice as high as in Germany, three times higher than France and six times that of the Netherlands.

Being a virgin until marriage is a vital asset, which youngsters should be proud of. Being a virgin generates self-esteem. Lack of self-esteem is due to absence of Christian education in the love of the Holy Spirit of Christ. The love of Christ in everyone is stronger than self-esteem. We must recognise our self-importance because we are created in the image and likeness of God.

The responsibilities and the consequences of teenager pregnancies should be shared by the Government, the Church, the Schools, parents, voluntary organisations and above all the teenagers themselves. Teenagers must be educated to know the love of Christ for them and the whole human race. The love of Christ in a teenager is stronger than the deprivation of any teenager.

The original sin weakened every aspect of human life. "All have sinned and lack God 's glory, and all are justified by the free gift of his grace through being set free in Christ Jesus." (Romans 3:23-24) JB.

Marriage and family life is on the decline because of idolisation of sexual activity and promiscuity or sex outside Marriage. Sex with another person whilst one of the parties is married destroys the Marriage at once on the ground of adultery.

Sexual drive is a gift of God. And it must not be abused; it should be rightly used under control by the holy partners at the right time.

Sexual activity must wait until after the wedding and after the "I do" is said by the partners. Marriage is a holy sacrament of the Church, the body of Christ.

"Be always humble, gentle, and patient. Show your love by being tolerant with one another. Do your best to preserve the unity, which the Spirit gives by means of the peace that binds you together. There is one body and one Spirit, just as there is one hope to which God has called you. There is one Lord, one faith, one baptism; there is one God and Father of all, who is Lord of all, works through all, and is in all." (Eph. 4: 2-6).

Love is God. Love comes from God through only Christ. Live your life in the Holy Spirit of Christ.

The matrimonial home is the abode of the Holy Spirit and a place of family worship and prayer. The family home must be kept holy by all members of the family and the whole world in the Holy Spirit of Christ. The sacrament of Marriage is for reconstruction and happiness.

13. Marriage and the Family under the Regime of Sin and Grace of God through Christ.

Sin is present in human history. Sin is rejection of God by a created being and opposition of God. Sin is an abuse of the freedom that God gives to created persons so that they may choose to love God and one another and not the Evil One.

Revelation in the Holy Bible gives us the certainty of faith that the whole of human life is affected by the original offence freely committed by our first parents, Adam and Eve.

Adam and Eve fell into sin through the seduction of a fallen angel called Satan or the Evil One and his demons. This Fall consists in the free choice of Satan and his demons, who radically and irrevocably rejected God and his reign.

They made the wrong decision. They joined the wrong army. The Evil One has sinned from the beginning and he is " a liar and the father of lies." *Jn 8: 44.*

Baptism washed away original sin and made the Christian the child of God. But original sin weakened human nature and the inclination to choose evil rather than good persists in human nature. The Evil One is within and around the family ready to create disorder.

According to faith the disorder does not stem from the nature of man or woman, nor from the nature of the marriage relations, but from sin brought about in the marriage and the family by the Evil One.

This disorder and the inclination to choose evil can be overcome in marriage and the family by the grace of God through persistent prayer in union with Christ. The spouses and the family should always seek self-renewal and self-knowledge through prayer.

The grace of God is powerful enough to enable the spouses and the family to achieve the goal of the marriage union for which God created man and woman to live in perpetual happiness in the beginning of the creation.

CHAPTER SEVENTEEN

Sacrament of Holy Orders for Renewal of the whole human race.

"But be brave! I have defeated the world" Jn 16: 33

Scriptural source of the Holy Orders. What is the sacrament of Holy Orders? The institution of the Church and the Mission of the Apostolic Ministry. Basic Essentials of Ordination in the Latin Rite. Essential Elements and Formalities of Ordination in the Latin Rite. Who can confer Holy Orders in the Latin Rite? Who can receive Holy Orders in the Latin Rite? Fruits and grace of Holy Orders.

Scriptural source of the Holy Orders.

The bishops with the priests as co-workers exercise the responsibility of preaching the Good News of Christ to the whole human race. This is evident when it was written:"Go throughout the world and preach the gospel to the whole human race. Whoever believes and is baptised will be saved; whoever does not believe will be condemned." *Mk 16: 15-16.*

What is the sacrament of Holy Orders?

Holy Orders is the sacrament through which the salvation mission entrusted by Christ to his twelve apostles continues to be carried out in the Church through the Pope, the head of the Church, the successor of St Peter, until the end of time. Thus, it is properly called the sacrament of apostolic ministry. It includes three degrees: episcopate, presbyterate and diaconate.

The episcopate and the presbyterate involve ministerial participation in the priesthood of Christ. The diaconate is intended to serve and help the sacramental ministry.

It is called "Orders" because the rite of *ordinatio* of the recipient means incorporation into an order, an *ordo.* Ordination is a liturgical action of consecrating the recipients into the ministry of the Church. Thus, the Latin liturgy expresses it in terms of *Ordo episcoporum,* the

Ordo presbyterorum, and the *Ordo diaconorum*. The word "ordination" is reserved for the sacramental action of the Church, which integrates a man into the Order of bishops, presbyters (priests) and deacons.

Ordination goes beyond a simple election, designation, delegation or institution by the community because it confers a gift of the Holy Spirit on the recipient. This gift empowers the recipient to exercise a sacred power (sacra potestas) in union with Christ and which comes direct from Christ himself through his Church. It is a call from Christ himself direct and not from the Church or the Community.

Ordination is called consecration (consecratio) because it sets apart the recipient by Christ himself to continue with his salvation works till he comes back.

The sacrament of Holy Orders like the sacrament of Marriage are directed towards salvation goal of Christ of the whole human race. Through the sacrament of Holy Orders and Marriage, the faithful, who had been consecrated through Baptism and Confirmation for the common priesthood of all the faithful, receives further particular consecration.

The Institution of the Church by Christ and the Mission of the Apostolic Ministry

Christ himself is the source, authority, mission and goal of the ministry of the Catholic Church. Holders of offices in the Church are invested with sacred power to promote the goals of the Church so that the human race may attain salvation through Christ.

Bishops exercise their ministry within the episcopal college in communion with the bishop of Rome, the successor of St Peter and head of the College. Priests exercise their ministry within the presbyterium of the diocese under the direction of their bishop.

Christ instituted the twelve apostles in the form of a College to study and carry out his salvation mission. This is evident in the Gospel according to Luke:

"When day came, he called his disciples to him and chose twelve of them, whom he named apostles: Simon (whom he named Peter) and his brother Andrew; James and John, Philip and Bartholomew, Matthew and Thomas, James son of Alphaeus, and Simon (who was called the Patriot), Judas son of James, and Judas Iscariot, who became the traitor." *Lk 6:13-16.*

Our Lord appointed Peter the "rock" of his Church and gave him the keys of the Church and instituted him the shepherd of the whole flock. This is evident when our Lord said:

"And so I tell you, Peter: you are a rock, and on this rock foundation I will build my Church, and not even death will ever be able to overcome it. I will give you the keys of the Kingdom of heaven; what you prohibit on earth will be prohibited in heaven, and what you permit on earth will be permitted in heaven." *Matt 16: 18-19.*

The pastoral responsibility of binding and losing was given to Peter and also to the College of apostles united to its head. This responsibility belongs to the Church's very foundation and is continued and preserved by the bishops under the primacy of the Pope, the bishop of Rome, Peter's successor.

The Pope is the perpetual and visible foundation of the unity both of the bishops and the whole members of the Church, the Body of Christ. The Pope has full, supreme and universal power over the whole Church of Christ. He is Vicar of Christ and pastor of the entire Church. He can exercise his power through Christ without any restriction.

The Pope exercises his authority through the episcopal College. Thus, the College has supreme and full authority over the universal Church of Christ. The episcopal College cannot exercise its power without the assent of the Pope.

Christ endows his Church's shepherd, the Pope with the "charism of infallibility in matters of faith and morals" to enable the Pope to continue the salvation mission of Christ.

The individual bishop is the visible source and foundation of unity in their own particular Churches in their district. The diocesan bishop is assisted by priests and deacons.

Basic Essentials of Ordination in the Latin Rite.

The Church of Christ came into being on Pentecost day when the Apostles were endowed and empowered by Christ with a special outpouring of the Holy Spirit coming upon them. By imposition of hands they passed on to their co-workers the gifts of the Holy Spirit, which is transmitted through episcopal consecration in the Church to our day.

Thus, by imposition of hands and through the words of the consecration, the recipient of the sacrament receives the Holy Spirit. The solemn prayer of consecration is said asking God to grant the recipient the grace of the Holy Spirit required for his ministry.

The following words of consecration are used whilst the bishop imposes his hands on the head of the recipient in the case of deacons:

"Lord, send forth upon them the Holy Spirit, that they may be strengthened by the gifts of your sevenfold grace to carry out faithfully the work of the ministry."

The words of consecration for priests are:

"Almighty Father, grant to these servants of yours the dignity of the priesthood. Renew within them the spirit of holiness. As co-workers with the order of bishops, may they be faithful to the ministry that they receive from you, Lord God, and be to others a model of right conduct."

The words of consecration for bishops are:

"So now pour out upon this chosen one that power which is from you, the governing Spirit whom you gave to your beloved Son, Jesus Christ, the Spirit given by him to the holy apostles, who founded the Church in every place to be your temple for the increasing glory and praise of your name."

Essential Elements and Formalities of Ordination in the Latin rite

Ordination takes place within the liturgy of the Holy Sacrifice of the Mass in the presence of the consecrating bishop. The initial rites are the presentation and election of the recipient, instruction by the bishop, examination of the recipient, litany of the saints, attesting that the choice of the recipient is made in keeping with the tradition and practice of the Church and the recipient is prepared for the solemn act of consecration.

There after the formalities vary as to each of the three degrees. In the case of deacons, who receive imposition of hands on their head not unto the priesthood, but unto the ministry, the formalities include giving them the book of the Gospel and the stole.

The priest is presented the paten and chalice, which are the symbols of offering, which he is called upon to present to God through Christ in the Holy Sacrifice of the Mass. He is anointed with holy chrism. This signifies special anointing by the Holy Spirit to give grace and make the priest's ministry fruitful. After the imposition of hands by the bishop, the priests who attend the ordination also impose their hands on the recipient one after the other.

The bishop is also anointed with the holy chrism like the priest. The bishop wears the priestly garments of his office, the pectoral cross and the dalmatic and receives the book of the Gospels, the ring, the mitre and the crosier. These are the signs of the bishop's apostolic mission to proclaim the Word of God, of his faithfulness to the Church, the bride of Christ, and his office as shepherd of the flock of Christ and the people of God. The bishop is finally led to the bishop's chair.

Who can confer Holy Orders in the Latin Rite?

Christ himself chose the apostles and gave them the authority to share in his salvation mission. Bishops who are validly ordained in the apostolic succession confer the three degrees of the sacrament of Holy Orders on the recipients.

Who can receive Holy Orders in the Latin Rite?

In the Latin Church, only men can receive Holy Orders and not women. This is because our Lord chose only men to form the College of the twelve apostles. The apostles in loyalty to Christ also chose men and co-workers to succeed them in their ministry. The Church considers herself bound by this choice made by Christ. On this score, the ordination of women is impossible in the Church.

The recipients in the Latin Church must also give promise of celibacy. They must also complete requisite studies. Priests must first receive the order of diaconate before ordination into the priesthood.

Bishops are drawn from the priesthood according to rules laid down by the Holy See.

No one has a right to receive the sacrament of Holy Orders, because the recipients are called to the vocation by God.

Fruits and Grace of Holy Orders

The sacrament of Holy Orders confers an indelible and permanent spiritual character on the recipient. It cannot be repeated or conferred temporarily to be withdrawn.

The grace of the Holy Spirit is received by the recipients to enable them to renew the whole human race by the bath of rebirth and to fulfil their call and ministry.

Our Lord is always seeking co-workers worldwide to receive the grace of the Holy Spirit for the ministry of his Church.

CHAPTER EIGHTEEN

Christian Funeral and Farewell Commendation to God

"Your Father already knows what you need before you ask him" Matt 6: 8

What is the Christian meaning of death? What is a Christian Funeral? The Christian Funeral is not a Sacramental. The Greeting of Faith of the Community. The Liturgy of the Word. The Eucharistic Sacrifice of the Mass. Farewell Commendation of the Soul of the Deceased to God.

What is the Christian meaning of death?

Christians believe there is everlasting life after death. Thus, the Christian meaning of death is revealed by God through the Paschal mystery of the death and Resurrection of Christ. In the death and Resurrection of Christ, reside our faith and hope: "I look for the resurrection of the dead and the life of the world to come."

Saint Paul expresses it more vigorously: " For we know that when this tent we live in – our body here on earth – is torn down, God will have a house in heaven for us to live in, a house he himself has made, which will last for ever. And now we sigh, so great is our desire that our home which comes from heaven should be put on over us; by being clothed with it we shall not be without a body.

While we live in this earthly tent, we groan with a feeling of oppression; it is not that we want to get rid of our earthly body, but that we want to have the heavenly one put on over us, so that what is mortal will be transformed by life. God is the one who has prepared us for this change, and he gave us his Spirit as the guarantee of all that he has in store for us.

So we are always full of courage. We know that as long as we are at home in the body we are away from the Lord's home. For our life is a matter of faith, not of sight.

We are full of courage and would much prefer to leave our home in the body and be at home with the Lord. More than anything else, however, we want to please him, whether in our home here or there.

For all of us must appear before Christ, to be judged by him. We will each receive what we deserve, according to everything we have done, good or bad, in our bodily life." *2Cor 5: 1-10.*

What is a Christian Funeral?

The moment of death ends the sacramental life and the earthly pilgrimage of a Christian. That moment opens a new door for the participation in the Lamb's wedding feast. We must be clothed in our nuptial garment ready to meet the bridegroom.

The Church, through the funeral liturgy, offers to God the soul of the deceased and commits to the earth the body that will rise in glory. The funeral liturgy is fully celebrated in the Eucharistic Sacrifice of the Mass.

The Roman liturgy offers three types of Christian funerals order, corresponding to the three locations at which the funeral can be conducted by choice of the family of the deceased: the home, the church and the cemetery.

In any location, the four main elements of the celebration are: the greeting of faith of the community, the liturgy of the Word, the Eucharistic Sacrifice of the Mass and a farewell to the soul of the deceased and final commendation to God for eternal life by the Church.

The Christian Funeral is not a Sacramental

The Christian funeral confers on the deceased neither a sacrament, a blessing or a sacramental because the decease has passed beyond the reach of the sacramental works of the Church. There is no sacramental or sacrament beyond because Christ himself is in charge beyond.

Sacramentals are sacred visible signs instituted by the Church, which resemble the visible signs of the seven sacraments. Sacramentals have the effect of making holy various occasions in life, persons, objects, places, meals et.c.

Celebration of sacramentals include a prayer and a specific sign, such as laying on of hands, the sign of the cross, the sprinkling of the holy water and exorcisms. Exorcisms are directed at driving out demons or liberation from demonic possession.

Among the sacramentals, blessings are the most important. The faithful Christians are always asking the priest to bless them before and after the Mass. These blessings are sacred actions of sacramentals of the Church.

Sacramentals do not confer the grace of the Holy Spirit as the seven sacraments do. The sacramentals only prepare the faithful to receive the grace of God through sanctification.

Popular piety, which enriches Christian life and faith, such as pilgrimages, visits to sanctuaries, veneration of relics, processions, the stations of the cross, use of medals, the rosary, religious dances, et.c. are not Christian funeral.

Sacramentals are derived from the baptismal priesthood. Thus, every baptized Christian is called to be a blessing, to bless and to love one another and enemies. Ask God to bless those who persecute you. Conquer evil by doing good to your enemies. Administration of sacramentals is generally reserved to bishops, priests and deacons.

The Greetings of Faith of the Community

The funeral celebration begins with greetings of faith. A welcome address to friends and relatives of the deceased with a word of hope in the Holy Spirit is made. All those who have died believing in everlasting life will rise to life. So we shall all be with the Lord.

The Liturgy of the Word

The readings from the Holy Bible should be carefully selected to fit the event. The homily of the priest should focus on the mystery of the death and resurrection of Christ.

The Eucharistic Sacrifice of the Mass

Here the family chose the celebration of the funeral in the church because they seek full Eucharistic Sacrifice of the Mass. The Church offers to God the Sacrifice of the death and Resurrection of Christ and prays that the deceased be purified of his or her sins and that he or she be admitted to the Lamb's banquet prepared for him or her through Christ. The Eucharist Mass enables communion, communication and prayer for and with the deceased by the Church, friends and relatives of the deceased.

Farewell Commendation of the Soul of the deceased to God.

The earthly pilgrimage has come to an end. The Christian Community expresses its last farewell to the deceased before the body is laid in the tomb – earth to earth, ashes to ashes and dust to dust.

Our Lord said:

> "I am the resurrection and the life.
> Those who believe in me will live,
> even though they die;
> and all those who live and
> believe in me will never die." *Jn 11: 25-26.*

A final commendation of the soul of the deceased to God is expressed – till we meet again.

CHAPTER NINETEEN

The New Vision in the Holy Sririt of Jesus Christ and Self-Renewal Through Faith in Jesus Christ. Use this Book Daily for the Gifts of the Holy Spirit, the Lord, the giver of Life and for Inspiration for Reconstruction

"And now I make all things new!" Rev. 21:5

- This book is inspirational, proactive, principle-based, morally and Spiritually educational for life. It is written for the whole human race in any trade, profession, vocation, employment and family in order to know the difference, which Jesus Christ makes firstly in changing and renewing the whole human race and secondly in order to improve the quality of life of the people of God worldwide.
- Throw yourself into the unconditional love of one another and the peace and tranquillity of Christ, who is the same from the beginning, today and forever.
- Awake your soul to the presence of God in order to share in the glory of God and everlasting life through Christ.
- Self-renewal is the wisdom of making holy one's physical, mental, emotional and spiritual nature in union with Christ in order to receive more energy and the grace of God and to respond effectively to one's daily responsibilities, vision and value driven goals. The message of Christ is for the whole human race for self-renewal.
- Deepen your understanding of faith in the Most Holy Trinity and in Jesus Christ and his salvation mission in order to have everlasting life.
- Understand the birth of Christ and how the virgin Mary's yes response to God changed the world through Christ.
- Understand what is faith in the living God in order to freely determine your own goals, vision and responsibilities and to build the kingdom of God on earth in union with Christ by using the tools of the wisdom of self-renewal.
- Fruits and grace of the sacrament of Baptism. Baptism of water and

Spirit washes away all your sins before Baptism.

- Fruits and grace of the sacrament of Confirmation in the Fellowship of the Holy Spirit. Be sealed with the Gifts of the Holy Spirit, the Lord , the giver of life.

  Our body is the temple of the Holy Spirit, who lives and moves in us by the Gift of God. We live in God, we walk in God, we are in God and we pray in God.

- The Holy Spirit gives us the grace of self-renewal in order to live a holy life controlled by the Holy Spirit, and not controlled by sinful human nature. The Holy Spirit gives us the grace to resist temptation through persistent prayer and practising life in the Holy Spirit of Christ. The Holy Spirit gives us the power to witness for Christ; to inform others about the Good News of Jesus Christ.

  The Holy Spirit inwardly transforms our life and helps us to conform ourselves to the standards and requirements of the Holy Spirit; we will not do what sinful human nature wants us to do but only what the Holy Spirit , the Lord, giver of everlasting life wants us to do.

- The rewards of life in the Holy Spirit of Christ are love, joy, peace, patience, kindness, goodness, faithfulness, gentleness and self-control. *(Gal 5: 16, 22-23).*
- Self-control means living upright, honest, pure, righteous, humble, forgiving, loving and faithful life in the Spirit of Christ; doing only what the Spirit instructs us to do and rejecting radically what human nature tells us to do.
- Fruits and grace of the sacrament of Reconciliation with God and with our neighbour and with our enemy and with those who persecute us. The rewards of Reconciliation are healing, health and forgiveness of sins for self-renewal and for improvement of the quality of life of the whole human race.
- The condition for receiving God's overflowing love and forgiveness is a true expression of our sorrow for our sins against our neighbour and God. The same overflowing love and forgiveness we receive from God should help us to forgive all persons who have hurt us and thus release all our pains and hurts into the endless love and forgiveness of God.
- Our God of love and forgiveness reveals himself to us when he said: "I, the LORD, am a God who is full of compassion and pity, who is not easily angered and who shows great love and faithfulness. I keep my promise for thousands of generations and forgive evil and sin." *(Exodus 34: 6-7).* That is the true and forgiving God of the

whole human race. Do not worship any other god, because we cannot worship God and money.

- Fruits and grace of the sacrament of the Eucharist, the Body of Christ given up for us and the Blood of Christ shed for us so that sins may be forgiven for self-renewal.
- Fruits and grace of the sacrament of anointing the Sick for health and healing.
- Fruits and grace of the sacrament of Marriage rooted in unconditional love for the people of God, faith in Christ and daily prayer for renewal of the people of God.
- Fruits and grace of the sacrament of Holy Orders for ministry and for renewal of the people of God.
- Enjoy life in the Spirit of Christ. Life in the Spirit of Christ means freedom from the Evil One and a non-resistance relationship with the world; love your enemies and those who persecute the Christ in you and pray for their interior conversion so that all of us together may become perfect as our Father in heaven is perfect.
- Preserve your freedom from the Evil One gained through Christ and know that after your death your soul cannot be reincarnated because everyone must live, die and be judged only once by God. *(Hebrews 9: 27).*
- Understand Christian funeral and commendation to God after the earthly pilgrimage and choose freely between Heaven or Hell for your destiny after death.
- Understand Life after death and the Particular and Last Judgement after death.
- Understand the mystery of the Resurrection of Christ to the Father and his second coming to raise to life the faithful and hand over the Kingdom of God to the Father and then the end will come. *(1 Cor 15: 23-26).*
- Understand freedom to choose happiness and to overcome stress and worry. Don't worry about tomorrow. Tomorrow will take care of itself. You have enough to worry about today. *(Mat 6: 34).*
- Understand self-knowledge and how to achieve your value-driven goals and vision. You should be quick to listen and slow to speak or to get angry. *(James 1:19).*
- Understand the principles of personal management of your talents, goals, vision and rewards and know that life in Christ is a practical daily action in union with Christ.
- Understand the origin of sin: the Evil One is the father of sin and

can be overcome by daily prayer and self-renewal through Christ.

- Sin weakens human nature; sin prevents contact and relationship between the sinner and God; sin undermines personal management of our talents, responsibilities, vision, rewards and freedom to choose.
- Pray daily for anything with thankful hearts and for self-renewal in secret whilst the door is shut for miraculous results through Christ. Pray for the fulfilment of the goals and vision of Human Freedom in union with Christ. God will bless you with peace that no one can understand. And this peace will guide the way you think, feel and express yourself.
- Understand the nature of prayer and how your prayers are answered in a state of self-renewal and humility through Christ, who is the messenger and the message of the living God, Light from Light and God from God.
- Before any goal, change, development, vision and improvement in the quality of life of the people in any community, politics, law and order, industry and commerce can be achieved, we must first change ourselves and respect human rights, which means human dignity or value, human freedom and faith in the living God and in Jesus Christ. *God created all of us, male and female, as his co-workers for building the kingdom of God on earth. Thus, you are special and important in the sight of God.*
- Do not be afraid of those who kill the body but cannot kill the soul; rather be afraid of God, who can destroy both body and soul in hell. For only a penny you can buy two sparrows, yet not one sparrow falls to the ground without your Father's consent. As for you, even the hairs of your head have all been counted. So do not be afraid; you are worth much more than many sparrows! *(Mat 10: 28-31)*
- Go away from me, Satan! You are an obstacle in my way, because these thoughts of yours don't come from God, but from human nature. *(Mat 16: 23).* That is the beginning of the new vision in the Spirit of Christ. That is the new vision of interior conversion for development and improvement of the quality of life of the whole human race. That is the vision of the people of God worldwide.
- If anyone wants to come with me; he must forget self, carry his cross, and follow me. For whoever wants to save his own life will lose it; whoever loses his life for my sake will find it. Will people gain anything if they win the whole world but lose their life? *(Mat 16:*

24-26).

- Watch out and guard yourselves from every kind of greed; because a person's true life is not made up of the things he owns, no matter how rich he may be. *(Luke 12:15).*
- Some people spend their money freely and still grow richer. Others are cautious, and yet grow poorer. Be generous, and you will be prosperous. Help others, and you will be helped. *(Proverbs 11:24-25).*
- I am the light of the world, Jesus said. Whoever follows me will have the light of life and will never walk in darkness. *(Jn 8:12).*
- We must invest in the whole human race created by God in the image and likeness of God through a transnational charity organisation in union with Christ. That is my vision for the way forward. What is your vision?
- The first principle of understanding is faith in the Most Holy Trinity and in Jesus Christ. *Life in the Holy Spirit of Jesus Christ* will guide you to achieve understanding, and your goal and vision in union with Christ.

The new vision

The new vision is discovery of human union with God; this means the human being shares in the nature of God. For that reason human beings cannot live on bread alone, but every word that God speaks.

Further, the word that God speaks is powerful enough to break through all limitations of the human being and to expand everyone to achieve one 's full potentials.

That union is inherent from the beginning of the creation; but human culture of servitude to ignorance, sin and death against God became a barrier to true knowledge and inspiration for reconstruction and happiness.

The dawn of true knowledge, love and truth through Jesus Christ has restored the human being to the full favour of God. What the Father can do through Christ, every human being can do it through Jesus Christ.

Jesus Christ has opened the gate of life and inspiration for reconstruction and happiness in every corner worldwide. The nature, of God, which the inhabitants of a country worship, constitutes the second to none infrastructure for the development of that country.

Human Freedom's Charitable Objects, Activities and Projects

HUMAN FREEDOM

Human Freedom means freedom from servitude to sin and death

[Reg. Charity No. 1049216 Reg. England No. 3087036 limited liability Company by Guarantee]
In association with Ave Maria Publishers Limited (AMP) Reg. England No. 4002569

Affiliated to the Ghanaian Catholic Chaplaincy in Britain

153 Temple Chambers, Temple Avenue, London, EC4Y 0HP
Tel: 020 7353 0133 **Fax: 020 7353 0533**

Human Freedom 's Charitable Objects

Human freedom 's charitable "objects are to promote general charitable purposes throughout the world and in particular to provide financial and other assistance for the advancement of education as the trustees in their absolute discretion may from time to time determine"

Activities and Projects of Human freedom

1. Protecting the human rights of the people together.
2. Integrating human rights law into business life
3. Promoting Business Centres in Ghana and Africa
4. Women 's health, education and employment for the stability of the family.
5. General charitable purposes, e.g. help for children, the aged, disabled, the poor, housing and medical aid.
6. Financing Nursing Homes, Convalescent Homes, and Fitness and Health Clinics .
7. Annual international human rights Festival, Prayer and Evangelisation in Britain and Ghana.
8. Regular human rights Conference, Prayer and Evangelisation of the people in the context of their culture for improving the quality of life of the people.
9. Distributing "Life in the Holy Spirit of Jesus Christ" (The Book for Life and Inspiration for Reconstruction) by Dr Robert K Glah, LL.M; Ph.D. [London]; Barrister; President, Human Freedom. (ISBN 1 903519 02 0) Softback (AMP) pp xxvi, 174
10. Distributing "Human Rights Law Everyone Should Know" (The vertical and horizontal vision of human rights law in the United Kingdom and in Europe) by Dr Robert K Glah, LL.M; Ph D [London]; Barrister; President, Human Freedom. (ISBN 1 903519 01 2) Softback (AMP) June 2001 in preparation
11. Distributing "Immigration and Human Rights Law in the United Kingdom" (AMP) (ISBN 1 903519 04 7) Softback by Dr Robert K Glah, LL.M; Ph.D [London]; Barrister; President, Human Freedom. June 2001 in preparation.
12. Distributing "Goal of International Investment" (ISBN 1 903519 05 5) Soft-back (AMP) in reparation June 2001

13. Distributing "Responsibilities of Company Directors in the Context of International Investment" (ISBN 1 903519 09 8) Softback (AMP) in preparation June 2001.
14. Establishing and financing the University of Christ the King (UCK) and a Christian education, housing and hospital complex in the Battor and Mepe traditional areas in the Volta Region, within the Archdiocese of Accra in the Republic of Ghana.

The Trustees of Human Freedom

Human freedom is an international human rights charity. All the trustees are Christians and it was founded to promote international human rights in union with our Lord Jesus Christ, the great human rights advocate of all seasons. The trustees invite you to share in the charity works of Human freedom by your gifts and prayers in union with our Lord Jesus Christ.

Contact: Mrs Ivy Amoako, Director, Human Freedom, (Reg. Charity No. 1049216) 153 Temple Chambers, Temple Avenue, London EC4Y 0HP.

Tel: 020 7353 0133 **Fax: 020 7353 0533**

Website: www.humanfreedomcharity.**org.uk**
E-mail:freedom @humanfreedomcharity.org.uk

Human Freedom (Ghana).

Human Freedom (Ghana) was incorporated in Ghana, Reg. No. G 7088, on 24th day of November 2000 with limited liability by guarantee with the same objectives and activities of Human Freedom incorporated in England and Wales in the United Kingdom.

General Secretary of Human Freedom

The General Secretary of Human Freedom in Ghana and worldwide is John K Bokor based in Ghana. The General Secretary, John K Bokor, is in the process of negotiating incorporation of Human Freedom in all African states and the rest of the world.

Trustees of Human Freedom (Ghana)

Mr Sampson Freeman Atani; Mr Andrew Yevu Bokor, Mr Raphael Kwami Ahiabenu and Miss Awo Veronica Agboyibor.

Contact: John K Bokor, Human Freedom, P O. Box 3895, Accra, Ghana.
Tel: 00 233 21 66 00 85
Fax/Tel: 00 233 21 66 43 97

E-mail us: book@avemariapublishersbooks. org. uk

Contact us: Ave Maria Publishers Limited
153 Temple Chambers
Temple Avenue
London EC4Y OHP

Tel: 020 7353 0133
Fax: 020 7353 0533

Basic Facts of 213 States and Countries of the World

	State/ Country	Date of UN Admission	Capital	Colonial Rulers	Population Est. UN
1.	Afghanistan	(19 Nov. 1946)	Kabul	-	20,883,000
2.	Albania	(14 Dec. 1955)	Tirane	-	3,650,000
3.	Algeria	(8 Oct. 1962)	Algiers	France	29,168,000
4.	American Samoa	-	-Pago Pago	U.S.A.	-
5.	Andorra	(28 July 1993)	Andorra		71,000
6.	Angola	(1 Dec. 1976)	Luanda	Portugal	11,185,000
7.	Anguilla	-	-	U.K.	-
8.	Antigua and Barbuda	(11 Nov. 1981)	Saint John's	U.K.	67,000
9.	Argentina	(24 Oct. 1945)	Buenos Aires	Spain	35,220,000
10.	Armenia	(2 Mar. 1992)	Yerevan	-	3,764,000
11.	Australia	(1 Nov. 1945)	Canberra	U.K.	18,289,000
12.	Austria	(14 Dec. 1955)	Vienna	U.K.	8,106,000
13.	Azerbaijan	(9 Mar. 1992)	Baku	-	7,554,000
14.	Bahamas	(18 Sep. 1973)	Nassau	U.K.	289,000
15.	Bahrain	(21 Sep. 1971)	Manama	-	599,000
16.	Bangladesh	(17 Sep. 1974)	Dacca	U.K.	120,000
17.	Barbados	(9 Dec. 1966)	Bridgetown	U.K.	265,000
18.	Belarus	(24 Oct. 1945)	Minsk		10,247,000
19.	Belgium	(27 Dec. 1945)	Brussels	-	10,159,000
20.	Belize	(25 Sep. 1981)	Belmopan	U.K.	222,000
21.	Benin	(20 Sep. 1960)	Porto Novo	France	5,514,000
22.	Bermuda		Hamilton	U.K.	53,000
23.	Bhutan	(21 Sep. 1971)	Thimphu	-	1,812,000
24.	Bolivia	(14 Nov. 1945)	La Paz	Spain	7,588,000
25.	Bosnia and Herzegovina	(22 May 1992)	Sarajevo	-	4,510,000
26.	Botswana	(17 Oct. 1966)	Gabarone	U.K.	1,490,000
27.	Brazil	(24 Oct. 1945)	Brasilia	Portugal	157,872,000
28.	British Virgin Islands	-	-	U.K.	-
29.	Brunei Darussalam	(21 Sep. 1984)	Bandar Seri Begawan	U.K.	300,000
30.	Bulgaria	(14 Dec. 1955)	Sofia	-	8,356,000
31.	Burkina Faso	(20 Sep. 1960)	Ouagadougou	France	10,870,000
32.	Burundi	(18 Sep. 1962)	Bujumbura	Germany/Belgium	6,088,000
33.	Cambodia	(14 Dec. 1955)	Phnom Penh	-	10,702,000
34.	Cameroon	(20 Sep. 1960)	Yaounde	France	13,560,000
35.	Canada	(9 Nov. 1945)	Ottawa	U.K.	29,964,000
36.	Cayman Islands	-	Georgetown-	U.K.	11,000
37.	Cape Verde	(16 Sep. 1975)	Praia	Portugal	396,000
38.	Central African Republic	(20 Sep. 1960)	Bangui	France	3,334,000
39.	Chad	(20 Sep. 1960)	N'djamena	France	6,515,000
40.	Chile	(24 Oct. 1945)	Santiago	Spain	14,419,000
41.	China	(24 Oct. 1945)	Peking	-	1,232,083,000
42.	Colombia	(5 Nov. 1945)	Bogotá	Spain	36,626,000
43.	Comoros	(12 Nov. 1975)	Moroni	France	632,000
44.	Congo	(20 Sep. 1960)	Kinshasa	Belgium	2,668,000
45.	Costa Rica	(2 Nov. 1945)	San Jose	Spain	3,398,000
46.	Côte d'Ivoire	(20 Sep. 1960)	Yamoussoukro	France	14,781,000
47.	Croatia	(22 May 1992)	Zagreb	Yugoslavia	4,501,000
48.	Cuba	(24 Oct. 1945)	Havana	Spain	11,019,000

49.	Cyprus	(20 Sep. 1960)	Nicosia	U.K.	756,000
50.	Czech Republic	(19 Jan. 1993)	Prague	-	10,315,000
51.	Democratic People's Republic of Korea (North)	(17 Sep. 1991)	Pyongyang	-	22,466,000
52.	Democratic Republic of the Congo	(20 Sep. 1960)	Brazzaville	Belgium	46,812,000
53.	Denmark	(24 Oct. 1945)	Copenhagen	-	5,262,000
54.	Djibouti	(20 Sep. 1977)	Djibouti	France	617,000
55.	Dominica	(18 Dec. 1978)	Roseau	U.K.	74,000
56.	Dominican Republic	(24 Oct. 1945)	Santo Domingo	Spain	8,052,000
57.	East Timor		Dili	Portugal	-
58.	Ecuador	(21 Dec. 1945)	Quito	Spain	11,698,000
59.	Egypt	(24 Oct. 1945)	Cairo	U.K.	60,603,000
60.	El Salvador	(24 Oct. 1945)	San Salvador	Spain	5,796,000
61.	Equatorial Guinea	(12 Nov. 1968)	Malabo	U.K./Spain	410,000
62.	Eritrea	(28 May 1993)	Asmara	-	3,280,000
63.	Estonia	(17 Sep. 1991)	Tallinn	-	3,280,000
64.	Ethiopia	(13 Nov. 1945)	Addis Ababa	-	58,506,000
65.	Falkland Islands (Malvinas)		Stanley	U.K.	3,000
66.	Fiji	(13 Oct. 1970)	Suva	U.K.	797,000
67.	Finland	(14 Dec. 1955)	Helsinki	-	5,150,000
68.	France	(24 Oct. 1945)	Paris	-	58,375,000
69.	Gabon	(20 Sep. 1960)	Libreville	France	1,106,000
70.	Gambia	(21 Sep. 1965)	Banjul	U.K.	1,141,000
71.	Georgia	(31 July 1992)	Tbilisi	-	5,411,000
72.	Germany	(18 Sep. 1973)	Bonn	-	81,912,000
73.	Ghana	(8 Mar.1957)	Accra	U.K.	17,832,000
74.	Gibraltar		Gibraltar	U.K.	-
75.	Greece	(25 Oct. 1945)	Athens	-	10,475,000
76.	Grenada	(17 Sep. 1974)	Saint George's	U.K.	99,000
77.	Guadeloup	-	Basse-Terre	France	335,000
78.	Guam	-	-Agana	U.S.A.	110,000
79.	Guatemala	(21 Nov. 1945)	Guatemala City	Spain	10,928,000
80.	Guinea	(12 Dec. 1958)	Conakry	France	9,518,000
81.	Guinea-Bissau	(17 Sep. 1974)	Bissau	Portugal	1,091,000
82.	Guyana	(20 Sep. 1966)	Georgetown	U.K.	838,000
83.	Haiti	(24 Oct. 1945)	Port-au-Prince	France	7,336,000
84.	Holy See	-	Vatican City	-	
85.	Honduras	(17 Dec. 1945)	Tegucigalpa	Spain	6,140,000
86.	Hungary	(14 Dec. 1955)	Budapest	-	10,193,000
87.	Iceland	(19 Nov. 1946)	Reykjavik	-	271,000
88.	India	(30 Oct. 1945)	New Delhi	U.K.	939,409,000
89.	Indonesia	(28 Sep. 1950)	Jakarta	Dutch	196,813,000
90.	Iran (Islamic Republic of)	(24 Oct. 1945)	Tehran	-	61,128,000
91.	Iraq	(21 Dec. 1945)	Baghdad	-	20,607,000
92.	Ireland	(14 Dec. 1955)	Dublin	-	3,521,000
93.	Israel	(11 May 1949)	Jerusalem/Tel Aviv	-	5,696,000
94.	Italy	(14 Dec. 1955)	Rome	-	57,399,000
95.	Jamaica	(18 Sep. 1962)	Kingston	U.K.	2,491,000
96.	Japan	(18 Dec. 1956)	Tokyo	-	125,761,000
97.	Jordan	(14 Dec. 1955)	Amman		5,581,000
98.	Kazakhstan	(2 Mar. 1992)	Alma-Ata		16,526,000
99.	Kenya	(16 Dec. 1963)	Nairobi	U.K.	31,806,000

100.	Kiribati	(14 Sept. 1999)	Bairiki	UK	75,000
101.	Kuwait	(14 May 1963)	Kuwait	-	1,687,000
102.	Kyrgyz Stan	(2 Mar. 1992)			4,575,000
103.	Lao People's Democratic Republic	(14 Dec. 1955)	Vientiane	France	5,035,000
104.	Latvia	(17 Sep. 1991)			2,078, 000
105.	Lebanon	(24 Oct. 1945)	Beirut	-	3,084,000
106.	Lesotho	(17 Oct. 1966)	Maseru	U.K;	2,078,000
107.	Liberia	(2 Nov. 1945)	Monrovia	U.S.A.	2,820,000
108.	Libyan Arab Jamahiriya	(14 Dec. 1955)	Tripoli	Italy	5,593,000
109.	Liechtenstein	(18 Sep. 1990)	Vaduz	-	32,000
110.	Lithuania	(17 Sep. 1991)		Soviet Union	3,710,000
111.	Luxembourg	(24 Oct. 1945)	Luxembourg	-	416,000
112.	Macan	-	Macan	Portugal	250,000
113.	Madagascar	(20 Sep. 1960)	Antananarivo	France	15,353,000
114.	Malawi	(1 Dec. 1964)	Lilongwe	U.K.	10,114,000
115.	Malaysia	(17 Sep. 1957)	Kuala Lumpur	U.K.	20,565,000
116.	Maldives	(21 Sep. 1965)	Male	U.K.	263,000
117.	Mali	(28 Sep. 1960)	Bamako	France	11,134,000
118.	Malta	(1 Dec. 1964)	Valletta	U.K.	373,000
119.	Marshall Islands	(17 Sep. 1991)	Saipan	U.S.A.	57,000
120.	Mauritania	(7 Oct. 1961)	Nouakchott	France	2,351,000
121.	Mauritius	(24 Apr. 1968)	Port Louis	France/U.K.	1,134,000
122.	Mayetta		Mamoundzou	-	-
123.	Mexico	(7 Nov. 1945)	Mexico City	Spain	96,578,000
124.	Micronesia (Federated States of)	(17 Sep. 1991)	Palikir	USA	111,000
125.	Monaco	(28 May 1993)	Monaco	-	32,000
126.	Mongolia	(27 Oct. 1961)	Ulaanbaatar	Russia/China	2,354,000
127.	Montserrat	-	-Plymouth	U.K.	12,000-
128.	Morocco	(12 Nov. 1956)	Rabat		27,623,000
129.	Mozambique	(16 Sep. 1975)	Maputo	Portugal	17,796,000
130.	Myanmar	(19 Apr. 1948)	Rangoon	-	45,922,000
131.	Namibia	(23 Apr. 1990)	Windhoek	U.K.	1,575,000
132.	Nauru	(14 Sept. 1999)	Yaren		9,000
133.	Nepal	(14 Dec. 1955)	Kathmandu	-	21,127,000
134.	Netherlands	(10 Dec. 1945)	Amsterdam/The Hague	-	15,517,000
135.	New Caledonia	-	-	France	-
136.	New Zealand	(24 Oct. 1945)	Wellington	U.K.	3,570,000
137.	Nicaragua	(24 Oct. 1945)	Managua	Spain	4,238,000
138.	Niger	(20 Sep. 1960)	Niamey	France	9,465,000
139.	Nigeria	(7 Oct. 1960)	Abuja	U.K.	115,020,000
140.	Norway	(27 Nov. 1945)	Oslo	-	4,381,000
141.	Oman	(7 Oct. 1971)	Muscat	-	2,302,000
142.	Pakistan	(30 Sep. 1947)	Islamabad	U.K.	134,146,000
143.	Palau	(15 Dec. 1994)	Koror	-	17,000
144.	Panama	(13 Nov. 1945)	Panama City	Spain	2,674,000
145.	Papua New Guinea	(10 Oct. 1975)	Port Moresby	Australia	4,400,000
146.	Paraguay	(24 Oct. 1945)	Asuncion	Spain	4,955,000
147.	Peru	(31 Oct. 1945)	Lima	Spain	23,945,000
148.	Philippines	(24 Oct. 1945)	Manila	Spain/USA	71,899,000
149.	Pitcairn	-		U.K.	
150.	Poland	(24 Oct. 1945)	Warsaw	Russia/Germany	38,618,000
151.	Portugal	(14 Dec. 1955)	Lisbon	-	9,808,000
152.	Puerto Rico	-	San Juan	Commonwealth with USA	c. 3,000,000
153.	Qatar	(21 Sep. 1971)	Ad-Dawhah	U.K.	558,000

154.	Republic of Korea (South)	(17 Sep. 1991)	Seoul	-	45,545,000
155.	Republic of Moldova	(2 Mar. 1992)	Chisinau	-Soviet Union	4,237,000
156.	Reunion Island	-	St Denis	France	-
157.	Romania	(14 Dec. 1955)	Bucharest	-	22,608,000
158.	Russian Federation	(24 Oct. 1945)	Moscow	-	147,739,000
159.	Rwanda	(18 Sep. 1962)	Kigali	Belgium	5,397,000
160.	St. Helen	-	Jamestown	U.K.	-
161.	Saint Kitts and Nevis	(23 Sep. 1983)	Basseterre/St. Kitts	U.K.	41,000
162.	Saint Lucia	(18 Sep. 1979)	Castries	U.K.	144,000
163.	Saint Vincent and the Grenadines	(16 Sep. 1980)	Kingstown	U.K.	113,000
164.	Samoa	(15 Dec. 1976)	Apia	U.S.A	166,000
165.	San Marino	(2 Mar. 1992)	San Marino	-	26,000
166.	Sao Tome and Principe	(16 Sep. 1975)	Sao Tome	Portugal	135,000
167.	Saudi Arabia	(24 Oct. 1945)	Riyadh	-	18, 000,000
168.	Senegal	(28 Sep. 1960)	Dakar	France	8,572,000
169.	Seychelles	(21 Sep. 1976)	Victoria	France/U.K.	96,000
170.	Sierra Leone	(27 Sep. 1961)	Freetown	U.K.	4,297,000
171.	Singapore	(21 Sep. 1965)	Singapore	U.K.	3,044,000
172.	Slovakia	(19 Jan. 1993)	Bratislava		5,374,000
173.	Slovenia	(22 May 1992)	Ljubljana	Yugoslavia	1,991,000
174.	Solomon Islands	(19 Sep. 1978)	Honiara	U.K.	391,000
175.	Somalia	(20 Sep. 1960)	Mogadishu	U.K.	9,822,000
176.	South Africa	(7 Nov. 1945)	Pretoria/Cape Town	Dutch	42,393,000
177.	Spain	(14 Dec. 1955)	Madrid/San Sebastian	-	39,270,000
178.	Sri Lanka	(14 Dec. 1955)	Colombo	U.K.	18,300,000
179.	Sudan	(12 Nov. 1956)	Khartoum	France	27,291,000
180.	Suriname	(4 Dec. 1975)	Paramaribo	Dutch	432,000
181.	Swaziland	(24 Sep. 1968)	Mbabane	U.K.	936,000
182.	Sweden	(19 Nov. 1946)	Stockholm	-	8,843,000
183.	Switzerland		Bern	-	6,500,000
184.	Syrian Arab Republic	(24 Oct. 1945)	Damascus	-	14,619,000
185.	Tajikistan	(2 Mar. 1992)	Dushanbe	Soviet Union	5,919,000
186.	Thailand	(16 Dec. 1946)	Bangkok		60,003,000
187.	The former Yugoslav Republic of Macedonia	(8 Apr. 1993)	Skopje	Yugoslavia-	2,163,000
188.	Togo	(20 Sep. 1960)	Lome	France	4,201,000
189.	Tokelau	-	-	New Zealand	-
190.	Tonga	(14 Sept. 1999)		U.K.	
191.	Trinidad and Tobago	(18 Sep. 1962)	Port of Spain	U.K.	1,297,000
192.	Tunisia	(12 Nov. 1956)	Tunis	France	9,092,000
193.	Turkey	(24 Oct. 1945)	Ankara	-	62,697,000
194.	Turkmenistan	(2 Mar. 1992)	Ashkhabad	Soviet Unio-	4,569,000
195.	Turks and Caicos Islands	-		U.K.	-
196.	Tuvalu	(5 Sept. 2000)			
197.	Uganda	(25 Oct. 1962)	Kampala	U.K.	19,848,000
198.	Ukraine	(24 Oct. 1945)			
199.	United Arab Emirates	(9 Dec. 1971)	Abu Dhabi		2,260,000
200	United Kingdom	(24 Oct. 1945)	London		58,784,000

201.	United Republic of Tanzania	(14 Dec. 1961)	Dodoma	U.K.	30,799,000
202.	United States of America	(24 Oct. 1945)	Washington D.C.	-	266,557,000
203.	United States Virgin Islands	-		U.S.A	-
204.	Uruguay	(18 Dec. 1945)	Montevideo	Spain	3,203,000
205.	Uzbekistan	(2 Mar. 1992)	Tashkent	-Soviet Union	22,912,000
206.	Vanuatu	(15 Sep. 1981)	Port Vila	France	169,000
207.	Venezuela	(15 Nov. 1945)	Caracas	Spain	22,311,000
208.	Vietnam	(20 Sep. 1977)	Hanoi	France	75,181,000
209.	Western Sahara	-	Laayoune	Spain	-
210.	Yemen	(30 Sep. 1947)	Aden/Sama	-	15,919,000
211.	Yugoslavia	(24 Oct. 1945)	Belgrade	-	10,574,000
212.	Zambia	(1 Dec. 1964)	Lusaka	U.K.	8,275,000
213.	Zimbabwe	(25 Aug. 1980)	Harare	U.K.	11,908,000

WORLD POLITICAL MAP

40°E
60°E
80°E
100°E
120°E
140°E
160°E
180°
160°W
80°N
60°N
40°N
20°N
0°
20°S
60°S
80°S
Spitsbergen (Norw.)
Novaya Zemlya
Finland
Helsinki
St. Petersburg
Moscow
Minsk
Kiev
Ukraine
Turkey
Ankara
Georgia
Syria
Beirut
Jerusalem
Cairo
Egypt
Baghdad
Iraq
Tehran
Iran
Ashkhabad
Kazakhstan
Astana
Tashkent
Kyrg.
Taj.
Kabul
Islamabad
Pakistan
New Delhi
Nepal
Katmandu
Bhutan
Bangladesh
Dhaka
India
Mumbai (Bombay)
Bangalore
Chennai (Madras)
Colombo
Sri Lanka
Maldives
Saudi Arabia
Riyadh
Abu Dhabi
U.A.E.
Muscat
Oman
Rep. of Yemen
Aden
Sudan
Khartoum
Asmara
Djibouti
Ethiopia
Addis Ababa
Somalia
Mogadishu
Kenya
Nairobi
Uganda
Kampala
Dem. Rep. of Congo
Tanzania
Dodoma
Malawi
Lilongwe
Zambia
Lusaka
Harare
Zim.
Mozambique
Maputo
Swaziland
Pretoria
Rep. of South Africa
Lesotho
Port Elizabeth
Madagascar
Antananarivo
Mauritius
Réunion (Fr.)
Seychelles
Arabian Sea
Bay of Bengal
Russia
Omsk
Tomsk
Novosibirsk
Yakutsk
Magadan
Anadyr
Kamchatka
Petropavlovsk-Kamchatskiy
Sakhalin
Khabarovsk
Ulan-Ude
Ulan Bator
Mongolia
China
Beijing (Peking)
Tianjin
Chengdu
Wuhan
Chongqing
Nanchang
Shanghai
Guangzhou
Hong Kong
Harbin
Vladivostok
N. Korea
Pyongyang
Seoul
S. Korea
Japan
Tokyo
Osaka
Kobe
Nagasaki
Sapporo
Taipei
Taiwan
East China Sea
Yellow Sea
South China Sea
Philippine Sea
Philippines
Manila
Cebu
Davao
Myanmar (Burma)
Yangon (Rangoon)
Vientiane
Laos
Thailand
Bangkok
Cam.
Phnom Penh
Vietnam
Hanoi
Malaysia
Kuala Lumpur
Singapore
Brunei
Sumatra
Indonesia
Jakarta
Bandung
Surabaya
East Timor
Darwin
Papua-New Guinea
Port Moresby
Coral Sea
Vanuatu
Fiji
New Caledonia (Fr.)
Micronesia
PACIFIC OCEAN
Tropic of Cancer
INDIAN OCEAN
Australia
Perth
Fremantle
Albany
Adelaide
Melbourne
Sydney
Canberra
Brisbane
Townsville
Tasmania
Hobart
Tasman Sea
Auckland
North Island
Wellington
South Island
New Zealand
Cro. Croatia
Cz. Rep. Czech Republic
Est. Estonia
Kyrg. Kyrgyzstan
Lith. Lithuania
Lux. Luxembourg
Mac. F.Y.R. Macedonia
Neth. Netherlands
Slo. Slovenia
Slov. Slovakia
Sw. Switzerland
Taj. Tajikistan
U.A.E. United Arab Emirates
Yugo. Yugoslavia
Zim. Zimbabwe
Modified Gall Projection
Equatorial Scale 1: 191,000,000
© Oxford Cartographers
+44(0) 1865 882884
Antarctic Circle
SOUTHERN OCEAN
ntarctica